BALANCING
THE
CHRISTIAN LIFE

·RYRIE'S·

BALANCING
THE
CHRISTIAN LIFE

MOODY PRESS
CHICAGO

This book is gratefully dedicated to some very special Dallas friends who have meant much to our family:

Phil and Martha Hook
Dwight and Dorothy Pentecost
Bob and Carolyn Schroeder
Charles and Leafa Tandy
Gene and Betty Wheeler
Ed and Gloria Yates

Copyright © 1969 by
THE MOODY BIBLE INSTITUTE
OF CHICAGO

Over 200,000 sold

31 32 Printing/LC/Year 92 91 90 89 88

ISBN: 0-8024-0452-9

Printed in the United States of America

CONTENTS

Part I: SOME BIBLICAL CONCEPTS

CHAPTER   PAGE

1. A Proposition 9
2. What Is Spirituality? 12
3. What Is Man? 24
4. The Old and the New . (. CONSCIENCE . ps . 4 2) 34
5. United with Christ 49

Part II: SOME PERSONAL RESPONSIBILITIES

6. How Are We Sanctified? 61
7. Dedication 75
8. Money and the Love of God 84
9. Using Your Gifts 94
10. Routine Faithfulness 102

Part III: SOME PRACTICAL PROBLEMS

11. How Can I Know if I Am Filled with the Spirit? 111
12. The Wiles of the Devil 123
13. Temptation 135
14. Confessing and Forgiving 144
15. Legal or Legalistic? 151
16. Should I Seek to Speak in Tongues? 163
17. Must Christ Be Lord to Be Saviour? 169
18. The Balanced Christian Life 182

PART I

SOME BIBLICAL CONCEPTS

1

A PROPOSITION

HERE IS A BASIC PROPOSAL or, if you wish, the thesis of this book: Genuine and wholesome spirituality is the goal of all Christian living.

It is possible that the very simplicity of the proposition might either deceive or at the least fail to make a proper impression on the one who reads it; so let us examine its key words.

By the word *genuine* I mean biblical, for only in the Bible do we have truth that is indisputably reliable. For this reason, the Bible must be the guide and test for all of our experiences in the spiritual life, for biblical spirituality is the only genuine spirituality. The practical importance of this is simply that all experiences of the spiritual life must be tested by biblical truth, and if any experience, no matter how real it may have been, fails to pass that test, it must be discarded. Of course, this is much easier said than done, but it is the only road to genuine or biblical spirituality.

A second key word in the original proposition is the word *wholesome*. By wholesome I mean balanced. There is nothing more devastating to the practice of spiritual living than an imbalance. One of my former teachers repeatedly reminded us that an imbalance in theology was the same as doctrinal insanity. The same applies to the realm of Christian living. An unbalanced application of the doctrines related to biblical spirituality will result in an unbalanced Christian life. Too much emphasis on the mystical may obscure the practicality of spiritual living, while an overemphasis on practicality may result in lack of vision. A constant reiteration of the need for repeated rededications could lead to a stagnant Christian life in which there is no consistent and substantial growth. An overemphasis on confession could

9

cause unhealthy introspection, while an underemphasis might tend to make one insensitive to sin. Balance is the key to a wholesome spiritual life.

If this is to be a book about spirituality, it is necessary at the outset to consider some general features of the word *spiritual*. The word is, of course, built on the root word for spirit and thus means "pertaining to spirit." Actually it has a rather wide range of uses, all of which are consistent with this basic idea of pertaining to spirit. (1) In one instance (Eph. 6:12) the word *spiritual* is used of the demonic hosts who, as spirit beings, are distinct from human beings. (2) In another usage the Mosaic law is characterized as being spiritual (Rom. 7:14). This reference indicates that the law was intended to have prospered the spiritual life of the Israelites to whom it was given. (3) The future resurrection body of the believer is termed a spiritual body in contrast to the natural body which he has until death (I Cor. 15:44). The use of the word in this connection forbids defining the word only in terms of the incorporeal. The spiritual body is one which like the Lord's after His resurrection has flesh and bones but which is of a new and different resurrection quality (Luke 24:39).

Furthermore, (4) a rather wide range of activities and relationships of the believer are called spiritual. His ministry is discharged through the exercise of spiritual gifts which are bestowed by the Holy Spirit (Rom. 1:11; I Cor. 12:1; 14:1). The unity of all Christians as stones in the building is designated a spiritual house by Peter who also states that believers are to offer up spiritual sacrifices acceptable to God (I Peter 2:5). The sustenance of the children of Israel was called spiritual meat and drink, and Christ is designated the spiritual "Rock" that followed them (I Cor. 10:3-4). The Christian expresses his praise in songs, hymns and spiritual songs (Col. 3:16). His mind is to be filled with spiritual wisdom (Col. 1:9), and his position in the heavenlies includes having been blessed with all spiritual blessings (Eph. 1:3).

However, the distinctive use (5) in the New Testament of the word *spiritual* is in connection with the believer's growth and maturing in the Christian life. A spiritual man must first of all be one who has experienced the regenerating work of the Holy

Spirit giving him new life in Christ. The Apostle Paul contrasts the spiritual man with the natural man (I Cor. 2:14-15), who, having not the Holy Spirit, is apparently an unregenerate individual (cf. Jude 19). But spirituality involves more than regeneration, and it is the purpose of this book to discuss these matters. This will of necessity involve studying certain doctrines of the Bible. Without this basis our conclusions might not lead to genuine spirituality. It will also demand consideration of certain individual responsibilities and practical problems in the outworking of biblical truth in the life in a balanced way. Too, it will be helpful to consider some contemporary misemphases in order to avoid the same pitfalls and in order to bring the truth into sharper focus. All of these matters should give a proper perspective on biblical spirituality.

It goes without saying (or does it?) that a subject like this one especially requires the teaching ministry of the Holy Spirit if it is to be learned fruitfully. Here is an area in which the need for proper balance can be illustrated. Some seem to feel that the teaching ministry of the Spirit overrides the need for study, while others conclude that sufficient study eliminates the need for the teaching ministry of the Spirit. The ministry of the Holy Spirit in teaching the truth of God is indispensable. But the Scriptures which speak of it (John 16:13; I Cor. 2:12) do not say that this ministry is always direct. In fact, nothing is said about the means the Spirit may use in order to teach us. It may be direct, as one quietly meditates on a passage, but it may also be through intermediate means. Some of these means are the books of men, the teachers given to the church, concordances and even English dictionaries. Ultimately it is the Spirit who does the teaching whether He chooses to use intermediate means or not. And He must do it if we are to grasp the truth.

2

WHAT IS SPIRITUALITY?

ODDLY ENOUGH, the concept of spirituality, though the subject of much preaching, writing and discussion, is seldom defined. Usually anything that approaches a definition merely describes the characteristics of spirituality, but one searches in vain for a concise definition of the concept itself. The reason for this is that the concept includes several factors, and it is not easy to weave these together into a balanced definition. Too, the only verse in the Bible that approaches a definition is rather difficult of interpretation: "But he that is spiritual judgeth all things" (I Cor. 2: 15). Consequently it is avoided. Nevertheless, it is necessary to try to formulate a definition, for this is like the cornerstone which determines the shape of the entire building.

THE CONCEPT OF SPIRITUALITY

Genuine spirituality involves three factors. The first we have already mentioned—regeneration. No one can be spiritual in the biblical sense without having first experienced the new life that is freely given to all who believe in the Lord Jesus Christ as personal Saviour. Spirituality without regeneration is reformation.

Second, the Holy Spirit is preeminently involved in producing spirituality. This is not to say that the other Persons of the Godhead do not have a part in it, nor that the believer himself has no responsibility, nor that there are not other means of grace; but it is to affirm His major role in spirituality. The ministries of the Spirit involve teaching (John 16:12-15), guiding (Rom. 8:14), assuring (Rom. 8:16), praying (Rom. 8:26), the exercise of spiritual gifts (I Cor. 12:7) and warring against the flesh (Gal. 5:17). All of these depend for their full manifestation on the filling of the Spirit (Eph. 5:18).

To be filled with the Spirit means to be controlled by the Spirit. The clue to this definition is found in Ephesians 5:18 where there is contrast *and* comparison between drunkenness and Spirit-filling. It is the comparison which gives the clue, for just as a drunken person is controlled by the liquor which he consumes, so a Spirit-filled Christian is controlled by the Spirit. As a result he will act in a manner unnatural to him—not an erratic or abnormal manner, but one contrary to the old life. Control by the Spirit is a necessary part of spirituality.

The third factor involved in spirituality is time. If the spiritual person judges or examines or discerns all things (I Cor. 2: 15), this must involve time in order to gain knowledge and to acquire experience for discerning all things. The Amplified Bible elaborates on the verse in this fashion: "He can read the meaning of everything, but no one can properly discern or appraise or get an insight into him." This could not be accomplished overnight; it is something which is true only of a mature Christian.

That word *maturity* seems to hold the key to the concept of spirituality, for Christian maturity is the growth which the Holy Spirit produces over a period of time in the believer. To be sure, the same amount of time is not required for each individual, but some time is necessary for all. It is not the time itself which produces maturity; rather, the progress made and growth achieved are all-important. Rate multiplied by time equals distance, so that the distance to maturity may be covered in a shorter time if the rate of growth is accelerated. And it will be accelerated if noꞏe of the control which ought to be given to the Holy Spirit is retained by self.

Here is a proposed definition of spirituality which attempts to be concise and at the same time to keep these above-discussed factors in mind. Spirituality is a grownup relation to the Holy Spirit. While this may simply be another way of saying that spirituality is Christian maturity, it tries to delineate more openly the factors of Spirit-control over a period of time. Certainly the definition satisfies the requirements of the description of a spiritual man in I Corinthians 2:15, for one who is experiencing a grownup relation to the Holy Spirit will be able to discern all things and at the same time will not be understood by others.

If this be a correct definition, there are certain ramifications of it which ought to be thought through.

1. A new Christian cannot be called spiritual, simply because he has not had sufficient time to grow and develop in Christian knowledge and experience. A new believer can be Spirit-controlled, but the area of control is subject to expansion in the normal process of Christian growth. A young Christian has not yet been confronted with many areas within the general sphere of Christian conduct, for instance; and while he may be completely willing to let the Spirit control his life and actions, he has not yet gained the experience and maturity that come from having faced these problems and having made Spirit-controlled decisions about them. When he is first saved he may not even know that there is such a person as a weaker brother and, although he may not be unwilling to curb his liberty for the sake of that brother, he has not yet faced the doing of it, to say nothing of having guided others into right decisions about such matters. Spirit-control may be total over the new Christian's life insofar as he has knowledge of that life in his newborn state, but as his knowledge increases and his growth progresses, new vistas of life break upon him which must also be consciously yielded to God's direction. Time to gain maturity is needed for genuine spirituality.

2. A Christian of longer standing may not be spiritual not because he has had insufficient time but because during the years of his Christian life he has not allowed the Holy Spirit to control him. Whereas the new Christian may lack the time required to become spiritual, the believer of longer standing may be deficient in yieldedness. And without complete and continued control by the Spirit he cannot be spiritual. This, of course, was the burden of the writer of the epistle to the Hebrews, for his readers were in this exact condition.

3. A Christian can backslide in certain areas of his life without losing all the ground he has gained during his Christian lifetime. The flesh may control his actions during a period of backsliding, but when he comes back to the Lord he does not necessarily have to start the process of growth all over again. For example, a believer may backslide with regard to personal Bible study, but when he comes back to it he will not have forgotten everything he formerly knew. However, this principle does not

apply in every area of life, for there are some aspects of living, such as fidelity in marriage, which if violated can never be fully redeemed. The sin can be forgiven, fellowship restored, but the ground lost cannot be recovered.

4. There are stages of growth within the area of maturity. The best illustration is that of the human being who, though in adulthood, continues to grow, develop and mature. The spiritual man who is experiencing a grownup relation to the Holy Spirit is not stagnant in his Christian life, for he also has a *growing* relation in his walk with the Lord. In this life we never ascend to a plateau above and beyond which there is no further ground to gain. Spirituality, then, is a growing, grownup relation to the Spirit.

5. The state of babyhood need not last long. Let no one try to take refuge in a fraudulent kind of piety which demeans or ignores the processes of growth that have advanced him to a state of maturity which he refuses to recognize. False humility is sometimes the reason for such lack of recognition of maturity which has actually been achieved. After all, when Paul wrote I Corinthians those believers were about four or five years old in the faith, and he expected them to be spiritual by that time. He makes it quite clear that although when he was with them he could not speak to them as spiritual people (for they were then babes in Christ), he fully anticipated that by the time he wrote this letter to them they would have matured to the point where he could address them as spiritual (I Cor. 3:1-2). With the passing of only a few years, babyhood should also disappear.

The Characteristics of Spirituality

Spirituality is more easily characterized than defined. And in the biblical characteristics of spirituality we have concrete tests by which one may determine whether or not he is spiritual. In fact, they are too specific for comfort! How can one know if he is spiritual? Here are the tests.

SPIRITUALITY WILL BE EVIDENT IN THE BELIEVER

In his character. If spirituality involves control by the Spirit (Eph. 5:18), and if the Spirit has come to glorify Christ (John 16:14), then a spiritual person will manifest Christ in his charac-

ter and actions. To glorify is to show, display or manifest. The evidence that the Holy Spirit is in control of a life is not found in manifestations of the Spirit but in the display of Christ. The fruit of the Spirit (Gal. 5:22-23) is a perfect description of the character of Christ; thus, the Christian who is spiritual will display love, joy, peace, long-suffering, gentleness, goodness, faithfulness, meekness and self-control. These are the traits that will describe his character.

In his conduct the spiritual believer will imitate Christ. One of the wrong emphases in victorious life teachings today demeans this aspect of the truth. We are told not to imitate Christ since this involves striving which is a work of the flesh; rather, we should simply allow Christ to live out His life through us. Actually it is not necessary to choose one of these views; both are scriptural. Christ lives in me, and the life I now live I live by faith in the Son of God (Gal. 2:20), but I am also exhorted to "follow his steps" (I Peter 2:21) and to walk as He walked (I John 2:6). Obviously if the Holy Spirit is allowed to produce the character of Christ in an individual, the life that he lives will imitate Christ. One of the most rewarding studies in the Gospels is to note the details of our Lord's life which we as His followers would do well to imitate. Here are some suggestions.

In His public life and ministry the Lord always exhibited compassion (Matt. 9:36; 14:14; 15:32; 20:34; Mark 6:34; 8:2; Luke 7:13). His love for people was always evident (Mark 10:21; Luke 19:41). He constantly offered to help others before being asked to do so (Mark 8:7; 12:15; Luke 13:12-13; John 5:6), ministering to both their physical and spiritual needs (John 6). He sought people out in order that He might bring God's message to them (Matt. 4:18; 9:35; 15:10; Mark 4:1; 6:2; Luke 4:14), and His ministry blessed the hearts of His hearers (Luke 24:32). The secret of such a public ministry is found in His personal life, for our Lord knew and used the Word of God (Matt. 4), and He constantly maintained fellowship with His heavenly Father through prayer (Matt. 14:23; Mark 1:35; Luke 5:16; 6:12; 9:18, 29; 11:1). These are some details of the pattern after which the spiritual Christian should mold his own life so that the glory of the Lord will shine from it. A spiritual Christian has a Christlike character and shows it in his Christlike conduct.

In his knowledge. The strong meat of the Word of God belongs to mature Christians (Heb. 5:14), and Paul expected the Corinthians after four or five years of Christian experience to be able to understand strong meat of the Word. The milk of the Word is for babes in Christ, and Paul did not scold the Corinthians for feeding on milk when they were first converted. But when their diet continued to consist only of milk, he, like the writer of the epistle to the Hebrews, denounced them as defective Christians. What is meat truth? Of course, the Bible does not label passages milk or meat, so it is not always easy to answer that question. However, one subject is clearly designated meat, and that is the matter which reminded the writer to the Hebrews of the inability of his readers to understand what he was writing about. And that subject is the truth about Melchizedek and his priesthood (Heb. 5:10-11). Here is an example from the Bible itself of the meat of the Word, and it may rightly be used as a test of one's spirituality. How much do you know about Melchizedek? Or, do you know any more about him now than you did a year ago? This is not an easy doctrine, admittedly, but it is a test doctrine for determining one's state of advancement in the knowledge of the Word of God which is an essential characteristic of genuine spirituality.

In his attitudes. A spiritual Christian will exhibit at least two basic attitudes throughout life. The first is an attitude of thankfulness. "Giving thanks always for all things unto God and the Father in the name of our Lord Jesus Christ" (Eph. 5:20). This admonition follows the command to be filled with the Spirit (v. 18) and is thereby one of the characteristics of a Spirit-filled life. It is to be an all-inclusive attitude in the life of the believer. It should apply at all times ("always") and in all situations ("for all things"). No time and no circumstance is excepted. This means that grumbling, carping criticism, discontent, etc. will not characterize a spiritual Christian. This does not mean he can never be discontent in the proper exercise of godly ambition nor that he should never criticize in the sense of exercising discernment (Phil. 1:9-10). But the kind of attitude that blames God for what we do not like or that is vexed with His dealings with us is not a characteristic of genuine spirituality.

The other attitude of life which characterizes the spiritual

Christian is, in the words of Paul, that of "endeavouring to keep
the unity of the Spirit in the bond of peace" (Eph. 4:3). This
is not entirely a positional matter; that is, it does not only relate to
the unity within the body of Christ which the Holy Spirit has
brought about by baptizing every believer into that body (I Cor.
12:13). It is true that we could never make such unity, but we
are exhorted to endeavor to keep it. The very fact that the word
keep is used shows that the unity has been made by the Spirit,
but the very fact that there is also an exhortation shows that we
must not disrupt that unity. Obviously, there is no problem about
keeping unity with members of the body of Christ who have pre-
deceased me; nor is there any difficulty in maintaining unity
with those other Christians whom I do not know or with whom
I have no contact. Therefore, the only sphere in which this exhortation has any relevance is the group of believers with whom
I am thrown in contact. And it goes without saying that there
are many practical problems in trying to keep the unity of the
Spirit among believers I know—and the same is true for believers
who know me! But, difficult as this may be, it is a requirement
of spirituality.

It was the lack of this attitude that called forth Paul's scathing
denunciation of the Corinthians (I Cor. 3:1-7; cf. 1:12-13). Dis-
unity had developed among believers who should have been worshiping together. Actually, there were four parties in Corinth
(1:12). The "Paul party" was perhaps a large group in the
church who had been converted under Paul and who continued
to adhere to him. But as is often the case they seemed disposed
to be more Pauline than Paul was and to disparage other gifted
men, all of which resulted in detracting from the glory of Christ.
The "Apollos party" (Acts 18:24-28) also contained some personal converts as well as those who had been won over by Apollos' genial manner and eloquent preaching. Some may have followed him because they considered his teaching more advanced
than Paul's plain gospel preaching or they were attracted to his
more cultured manner. The "Peter party" would undoubtedly
have been composed of conservative Jewish believers who rallied
to the hero of Pentecost. The "Christ party" was perhaps the
most difficult to get along with, for those in this group prided
themselves on being His followers, not any mere man's disciples.

They were Gnostics before Gnosticism, and they unquestionably strutted their supposed spiritual superiority before all. This is the kind of situation, attitude and activity that Paul unhesitatingly labeled "carnal" (I Cor. 3:3), for it broke the unity of the Spirit.

However, unity is an area in which there needs to be very carefully balanced thinking, for all division is not necessarily wrong, and all unions are not *per se* right. In the same epistle (11:19) Paul said: "For there must be also heresies among you, that they which are approved may be made manifest among you." The noun *heretic* is used only one time in the New Testament (Titus 3:10), but the noun *heresies* is used twice (here and Gal. 5:20 where the action is condemned as a work of the flesh). The word means a willful choosing for oneself which results in a party division. Even though heresy is a work of the flesh which is often performed by a carnal Christian, it may be used for good so that those who are not involved in heresy will stand out in the churches. But heresy seems to involve the espousal of error which in turn causes the division. In such instances the heretic is to be admonished twice, then ignored (Titus 3:11) while the part of the divided group that did not follow the error goes on demonstrating its purity of doctrine by abounding in the work of the Lord. Thus to put in balance I Corinthians 3:1-5 and 11:19 we may conclude: Divisions involving heresy may be good and necessary, but divisions over personalities are carnal.

On the other hand, some aspects of unity need to be carefully thought through. For one thing, unity does not necessarily imply bigness. The unity of the church was apparently not broken when the disciples were scattered by persecution (Acts 11:19). Unity existed between the church in Jerusalem and the church in Antioch even though they were separated geographically (Acts 11: 22-23). Unity was demonstrated by many churches who participated in the collection for the saints in Judea (II Cor. 8:1 ff.). The unity of the one church in a given city in New Testament times was not violated by the fact that there were several churches meeting in houses scattered about the city. Indeed, one receives the impression from the New Testament that the Lord preferred to have many smaller congregations rather than one large group

in any given place. And there seemed to be no lack of power
that stemmed from lack of bigness.

Furthermore, the expression of personal preferences or use of
various procedures does not necessarily violate the unity of the
church. Indeed, it is in the use of a variety of spiritual gifts that
the unity of the body is maintained and the progress of the body
furthered (I Cor. 12:12-25). Paul may have preferred Silas while
Barnabas desired Mark (Acts 15:39-40), but eventually Paul
recognized Mark's value in the ministry (II Tim. 4:11). Honest
differences of opinion can be expressed within the bonds of the
unity of the body of Christ.

The two basic attitudes of life that must characterize genuine,
biblical spirituality are thankfulness at all times and in all circumstances and the maintenance of unity in that part of the
body of Christ with which I live and am concerned—with all of
their implications.

In his conduct. Spirituality is also demonstrated in the individual by proper conduct which is the result of the correct, discerning and mature use of knowledge (Heb. 5:13-14). We have
already noticed that knowledge of the Word including meat
truth is a prerequisite for spirituality, but such knowledge must
be used properly in order to be spiritual. The readers of the
book of Hebrews were unskillful in the word of righteousness
(v. 13); that is, the word concerning uprightness in both doctrine
and practice. As a result they were unable to discern between
good and evil (v. 14). This should not be limited to things
morally good or evil, but extended to things superior versus things
inferior, things better versus things which are best. A spiritual
Christian will be able to tread his way carefully through the complexities of Christian living so that he not only does that which is
right and scriptural but also that which is useful and for the
good of others. Notice that in the foregoing passage again time
is involved in maturity or spirituality. These people had had time
to exercise their spiritual senses though they had not done so.
But time is required to reach this state and achieve the ability to
use skillfully God's Word.

SPIRITUALITY WILL BE SEEN IN THE BELIEVER'S HOME

The easiest place in which to be spiritual is in public; the

most difficult is at home. The relationships of the home are inti-
mate and continuous, while activities and impressions made in
public are intermittent and casual. This axiomatic reminder is
especially necessary for Christian workers who too often can
make a show of professional spirituality in public ministry while
living a carnal life at home.

Let me illustrate by changing the comparison slightly. When I
first began to teach I was assigned a beginning class in New
Testament Greek which met every morning, Monday through
Friday, at eight. During the course of an academic year under
circumstances like that, one gets well acquainted with students
in such a class—and they with the teacher. Now if, at the end of
the year, members of that class should testify how much their
teacher's life, ministry and spiritual example had meant to them,
it would mean a great deal. But, by contrast, if I go to a church
on a single occasion and preach a fine message to the congregation, and after the service certain ones tell me how spiritual I
must be to preach such a sermon, that means nothing in reality.
In the case of the class, they have come to know and observe me
under varying circumstances of stress and joy; they have been
able to observe constantly my patience (or lack of it) and my
consistency. But the casual contact with a congregation affords
no opportunity to assess the spirituality of the minister. The circumstances of homelife afford an even better opportunity than
a daily 8:00 A.M. Greek class.

Again it is the Ephesian passage concerning the filling of the
Spirit (5:18-21) which provides the biblical basis for this characteristic of spirituality. The command to be filled with the
Spirit (v. 18) is followed by four coordinate phrases each of
which begins with a participle. Together they constitute results
or characteristics of the Spirit-filled life. The four participles are
speaking, singing (v. 19), giving thanks (v. 20), and submitting
(v. 21); and the last is not only the conclusion to verses 18-21
but it is also the topic sentence to that which follows beginning
in verse 22. In other words, submission which is an evidence of
the filling of the Spirit will be seen in the relationships of the
home most vividly.

The word *submit* means to place oneself in a subordinate rank.
This means distinctive things for the husband and for the wife

in the home, but both are to be submissive to one another (not just the wife to the husband as is commonly taught). For the husband it involves at least three things: (1) He is to lead, for he is the head of the wife (v. 23). This does not make him a dictator, but the responsible leader of the family who not only has the privilege of making the final decision but also the responsibility. (2) He is to love his wife (v. 25). A man needs this reminder, for he by nature is prone to be less demonstrative if not less loving than a woman. (3) He is to nurture his wife (v. 29). The word translated "nourish" means to bring to maturity and is used in the New Testament only in this verse and in 6:4. The word *cherish* means to warm and is used here and in I Thessalonians 2:7 only in the New Testament. The point is simply that the husband is ultimately responsible for helping bring to spiritual maturity his wife and family. The contemporary tragedy is simply that usually the opposite is the case. It is too often the wife who is spiritually astute and who is forced, so to speak, to pull her husband along. Both should be spiritually keen, and it is the husband's responsibility to take the leadership in this most important matter.

The spiritual wife will be subject to the leadership of her husband (vv. 22, 24). In other words, she will not work at cross purposes with her husband's leadership in the family. This does not mean that she has no voice, for the husband is as a presiding officer over the members of the family (that word is used in I Tim. 3:4). Of course no one can produce spirituality in another, but it is the awesome responsibility of the husband in the family to take the initiative and provide the leadership in the spiritual life of the family. Thus the spirituality of an individual will be seen in the proper discharge of his family responsibilities.

SPIRITUALITY WILL BE SEEN IN THE BELIEVER'S CHURCH FELLOWSHIP

The other principal area in which personal spirituality will be demonstrated is the church. We have already seen that a spiritual person will try to keep the unity of the Spirit in the sphere with which he is chiefly concerned—his own local church. A factious spirit is evidence of carnality.

The positive contribution a spiritual Christian will bring to the church is through the exercise of his spiritual gifts. We want

to consider this entire matter in detail later, so at this point it will have to suffice simply to point out that a spiritual believer will exercise his spiritual gifts in the power of the Holy Spirit in relation to the church universal and local. The immature Christian promotes division; the mature one, unity through the use of his gifts (I Cor. 12:25). It goes without saying, then (or does it?), that the church member who is always creating problems and who constantly demands to be catered to is not a genuinely spiritual person. But the one who is serving the Lord by promoting the welfare of the church is evincing a mature spiritual life. Accusing the brethren is the work of the devil (Rev. 12:10); caring for the brethren is the work of the Lord through His mature children.

This is genuine and wholesome spirituality. The concept is that of a mature and maturing relationship to the Holy Spirit which will be demonstrated in one's personal life, family life and church life. This is biblical spirituality.

3

WHAT IS MAN?

IT IS THE CHRISTIAN MAN whom God is trying to make spiritual, and spirituality is demonstrated only through human beings. Neither angels nor animals are capable of spiritual development; therefore, certain aspects of the nature of man are important in understanding true spirituality. It is necessary, then, to examine some features of the nature of man which bear upon spirituality.

MAN IS CREATED

The biblical teaching that man is a created being has important ramifications in the consideration of spirituality. The alternative to creation is evolution. If man evolved, there is really no need for a Saviour, regeneration, a new nature or supernatural help in living a good life. If he has come all the way that evolution claims he has by means of natural processes, what need has he for supernatural interference in his existence? Natural forces have served him well. God would only be an unnecessary addendum to his development. Of course, by God I mean the God of the Bible who is revealed there and who became incarnate in Jesus Christ. This God is unnecessary in the evolutionary picture, although a god of man's own making is not only compatible with the evolutionary dogma but is often a part of that system. The true God is unnecessary although even He may be included accidentally.

On the other hand, if man was created and (anticipating the next section) if he has fallen into sin, then he needs supernatural intervention in order to rescue him from this state and enable him to live a life pleasing to God. The doctrine of the creation of man carries with it the corollary concept of the responsibility of man. If God created man then there is someone outside of

24

man to whom he becomes responsible. He is not in and of himself the master of his own fate; he is neither the final authority nor the only one to whom he must finally answer. A Creator implies responsible creatures—responsible to that Creator.

But is there not a third option, theistic evolution? Theistic evolution (that is, that God created the first life, then natural evolution took over) is a popular viewpoint, but actually it furnishes no new alternative to those already stated. For if God "created" all things through the use of processes of evolution, then it is quite conceivable that man could be redeemed or at least live the "Christian" life by means of natural processes as well. Theistic evolution seems to be popular chiefly with those who want to choose what parts of the Bible they will accept plainly and what other parts they will allegorize. In this way the "thrust" of the Bible can be accepted ("Genesis 1 tells us *who* the Creator is, not *how* He created") without acknowledging the details of that revelation ("But *couldn't* God have done it through evolution?").

Actually theistic evolution is not acceptable either to the Bible-believing Christian or to the evolutionist—only to the theistic evolutionist! The Bible states clearly that man was created out of the dust of the ground (Gen. 2:7). Furthermore, the first man of the Bible was made in the image of God and thus bears no resemblance to evolution's first men. Evolutionists, too, do not accept the idea of theistic evolution for the simple reason that to admit supernaturalism at any point is to counter directly their theory. Julian Huxley affirmed that supernaturalism "runs counter to the whole of our scientific knowledge. . . . To postulate a divine interference with these exchanges of matter and energy at a particular moment in the earth's history is both unnecessary and illogical."[1] Thus the fact of man's creation focuses attention on the fact of and need for supernatural intervention and upon the responsibility of the creature to please his Creator.

MAN IS FALLEN

The truth of the fall of man is, of course, the other side of the coin of the fact of his creation by God, and it has many important consequences in the matter of spirituality.

1. Julian Huxley, *Evolution in Action,* p. 20.

Not all believe that the fall was a historical event even though they may acknowledge the fact of sin. But a nonhistorical view of Genesis 3 cannot help but blur the detail of the consequences of sin listed in that chapter. One writer says,

> Unless we are invincible fundamentalists, we know that Gen. 3 is properly to be regarded as "a true myth"—that, though Eden is on no map and Adam's fall fits no historical calendar, that chapter witnesses to a dimension of human experience as present now as at the dawn of history—in plain terms, we are fallen creatures, and the story of Adam and Eve is the story of you and me.[2]

This is simply an attempt to try to preserve the fact of sin without the fall of man and to dull the consequences of sin which are linked in the historical account of Genesis 3 with that fall.

Genesis 3 records an actual, historical event—the most consequential one in all human history. The tempter's method was very clever. His lure was this: "Yea, hath God said, Ye shall not eat of every tree of the garden?" The emphasis in his voice was undoubtedly on the word *every*. We gather this from the reply which first came to Eve's mind: "We may eat of the fruit of the trees of the garden." Satan's bait was to try to get Eve to think of the fact that God should give them everything. In other words, he was planting in Eve's mind the idea that there should be no restrictions in the perfect plan of a good God. Eve's reply showed she felt that for all practical purposes God had given them everything: "We may eat of the fruit of the trees of the garden" or, in other words, "Of course, God has given us everything." Only then did it occur to her that there was one restriction; so she added, almost as an afterthought, "But of the fruit of the tree which is in the midst of the garden, God hath said, Ye shall not eat of it, neither shall ye touch it, lest ye die." The important thing to notice in this part of her answer is that Eve's thoughts had begun to center on the restriction in God's plan.

Having taken Satan's bait and having begun to concentrate on the restriction in God's plan, Eve was then softened up for the next phase of the attack. "And the serpent said unto the woman, Ye shall not surely die: for God doth know that in the day ye eat thereof, then your eyes shall be opened, and ye shall be as gods,

2. Archibald M. Hunter, *Interpreting Paul's Gospel*, p. 77.

knowing good and evil." Of course Satan did not inform Eve
that if she followed him her life would be shortened and she
would become like the devil himself. He promised her that she
would be like God.

Eve's next step was to begin rationalizing the wrong she was
about to commit. She began to examine the forbidden fruit and
to point out to herself all the good things about it. After all, she
reasoned, wasn't it good for food, and did not God want them to
eat good food? And shouldn't a woman particularly be desirous
of setting good food before her husband? Wasn't this her God-
given responsibility? She also reflected on its beauty, and applied
the same line of argument. Why should God, who obviously
created a beautiful world, withhold something beautiful from her?
Too, if wisdom is desirable and if the fruit could make one wise,
then it must be desirable to eat that fruit. Gone from her mind
now was the central and all-important fact that God had expressly forbidden the eating of the fruit of that tree. Her mind
was filled only with rationalizations and, having thus prejustified
her action, Eve ate in flagrant disobedience to the revealed will
of God.

Many consequences flowed from this act—consequences to
the serpent, to the ground, to women, but chiefly (as far as our
purpose in this discussion is concerned) to the race. When
Adam and Eve ate that fruit they immediately experienced death
as God had warned. Death is not extinction in any uses of the
word. It is always separation. The moment the first parents
ate, they became separated from God. They sensed this, for their
avoidance of God's fellowship shows this quite vividly. Since
like breeds like, their children were born in a state of spiritual
death or a state of separation from God, and the actions of the
first child proved that all too clearly (Gen. 4:4, 8).

The New Testament abundantly affirms the historicity of the
fall of Adam and the consequence of spiritual death. Our Lord
considered Adam a historic person who actually lived at the beginning of human history (Matt. 19:4). That Satan beguiled
Eve is affirmed by Paul in II Corinthians 11:3. That a transgres-
sion was committed is clearly stated in I Timothy 2:14, and this
sin brought spiritual death to all the human race according to
Romans 5:12: "Wherefore, as by one man sin entered into the

world, and death by sin; and so death passed upon all men, for that all have sinned." The parallelism of this passage (Rom. 5: 12-21) is particularly striking. The apostle contrasts the one man Adam with Christ; his act of sin with our Lord's act of substitution; and the result of condemnation in Adam with justification for all who believe in Christ. This may be charted for clarity:

One man (Adam)	*One Man* (Christ)
One act (eating the fruit)	*One act* (dying in our place)
One result (condemnation for all)	*One result* (justification for believers)

If you remove the historicity of Adam from your theology (as Barthians and liberals do), then what is left of the parallelism? If you deny the actuality of the fall with its consequence of spiritual death, what have you done to the parallelism? Conversely, if you accept the historicity of Jesus Christ and the actuality of His death, then it follows that a real Adam who did a certain thing also lived. You cannot have one without the other.

If man is a created and a fallen being, as these two propositions assert, then a very specific kind of foundation is laid on which to build one's doctrine of spirituality. If, by contrast, man is evolving and progressing morally along with it, the biblical doctrine of spirituality becomes meaningless. In other words, if natural forces produced man and if whatever badness there may have been in primitive man is being erased through knowledge and progress, there is little, if any, place for supernaturalism. Regeneration of the person by God, a life lived in dependence on the unseen Holy Spirit, and all the facets of supernatural Christianity become unnecessary.

This antisupernatural viewpoint was expressed in a popular way (even though the "Supreme Being" is given a polite nod) in an article which appeared some time ago in the *Reader's Digest*. It is entitled "Upward!" and it supposedly traces man's evolutionary progress. It needs only to be updated today by the mention

of man's feat in putting himself into outer space. Otherwise it is, unfortunately, the typical and contemporary image most people have of man's "upward climb." It is cast in the form of a drama which is nearing its climax:

> Act One: From some ancestral cathedral of energy in the cold, black void of the eternal universe came the speck of matter, the sun, and its offspring, the earth.
>
> Act Two: From that speck of matter came a living cell and then multicelled organisms beneath the sea. From that sea, climbing that first inch upward, the amphibian, then the reptile and the bird, and with the bird, the first limited probing of outer space.
>
> Act Three: Another branch, the mammal, developing a brain, an ability to use tools and eventually a soul, forged the means to propel itself off the ground a few feet at Kitty Hawk, then a mile toward outer space. Then ten. Then 20. . . . Reconnoitering the unknown, man has tossed a tentative satellite a thousand miles out into space along the far road back to his origin. . . .
>
> Perhaps to that Supreme Being, the clock is now ticking off the final seconds in man's struggle to rise upward in body and spirit through time and space toward the mysterious source whence he came.[3]

The two important points to notice are (1) man's soul as well as his body evolved by means of natural causes, and (2) man through scientific means is attaining to supernatural status. Such concepts are diametrically opposed to the biblical teaching of the creation of man and of his fall from a perfect state to a sinful state (rather than his rise from an ignorant to a perfect state).

MAN IS SINFUL

Once a leading medical doctor attending a psychiatric convention in the author's home city declared: "There is no place for the concept of sin in psychotherapy. To introduce this concept is highly precarious. No human being should ever be blamed for anything he does." Suppose a colleague at the same convention had risen to his feet and declared: "There is no place for the concept of disease in medicine. To introduce this concept is highly

3. Beirne Lay, Jr., "Upward!" *Reader's Digest* (Mar., 1958), p. 224.

precarious. No human being should ever be blamed for being
a carrier of disease." He would have been laughed out of the
auditorium. The symptoms of disease are apparent everywhere,
and without acknowledging the cause there is not much chance
of effecting a cure. So it is also with sin. And yet throughout
history men have tried to ignore, tone down or eliminate the idea
of sin.

What is sin? Some have declared it to be a lack of knowledge
or a lack of a sufficiently evolved state of moral progress. Others
have been more theological and have defined sin as selfishness.
This is a good definition as far as it goes, but the difficulty with
it is that it does not cover all cases. Although most sins partake
of the character of selfishness, there are some instances of un-
selfish sinning. One could conceive of a case where a theft is
committed for no selfish purpose, and yet stealing is a sin. Was
an outlaw like Robin Hood not a sinner even though he stole from
the rich and gave to the poor?

The biblical definition of sin is that it is lawlessness (I John
3:4). This is a very simple definition but it encompasses far more
than meets the eye. To understand sin according to this definition we must define law, for unless we understand the standard,
we will not know what the deviations from that standard are.
What is law? The answer to that depends on what period of
human history you are thinking about. Law in the Garden
of Eden was one thing; law in the time of Abraham consisted of
certain specific ordinances and statutes (Gen. 26:5). In the time
of Moses, law was contained in the 613 commandments of the
Mosaic code which God gave through him to the Israelites. Today law means the hundreds of specific commandments of the
New Testament, and deviation from any of these is sin according
to the definition. Actually all of the commandments and principles of the New Testament stem from the one all-inclusive principle of I Corinthians 10:31: "Whether therefore ye eat, or drink,
or whatsoever ye do, do all to the glory of God." Sin is coming
short of the glory of God (Rom. 3:23).

Sin is universal. "All have sinned" (Rom. 3:23; 5:12). "There
is none righteous, no, not one: there is none that understandeth,
there is none that seeketh after God" (Rom. 3:10-11). "Behold,

I was shapen in iniquity; and in sin did my mother conceive me" (Ps. 51:5). "And you hath he quickened, who were dead in trespasses and sins; wherein in time past ye walked according to the course of this world, according to the prince of the power of the air, the spirit that now worketh in the children of disobedience: among whom also we all had our conversation in times past in the lusts of our flesh, fulfilling the desires of the flesh and of the mind; and were by nature the children of wrath, even as others" (Eph. 2:1-3). Two facts emerge from such verses: all have sinned in act or deed, and all are by nature sinners.

But the question most relevant to the matter of spirituality is Does the Christian sin? The answer is in the affirmative and encompasses all believers. Even the Apostle Paul remarked toward the end of his life and as a spiritually mature person, "Christ Jesus came into the world to save sinners; of whom I am chief" (I Tim. 1:15). Or listen to the testimony of another mature apostle of great experience in the Christian life. John wrote: "If we say that we have no sin, we deceive ourselves, and the truth is not in us. If we confess our sins, he is faithful and just to forgive us our sins, and to cleanse us from all unrighteousness. If we say that we have not sinned, we make him a liar, and his word is not in us" (I John 1:8-10). There are three confessions in these verses. The first is the confession of the principle of sin (v. 8). By this John means admitting that we possess the root of sin in contrast to specific acts of sin. If we—and he is writing to Christians (notice "my little children" in 2:1)—do not admit the presence of the sin nature, we only lead ourselves astray and the truth is not in us. We live in an atmosphere of self-made darkness. The second is the confession of particular sins (v. 9). To confess a particular sin means to say the same thing about it as God does, and this may cost something. The third is the confession of personal sins (v. 10). One may admit the truths of verses 8 and 9 in the abstract but never admit being personally involved in sin. To take this course of action is to make God a liar and to prove that His word is unknown to us. These words written to Christians show very clearly that all are sinful and that no believer, however spiritual or mature, ever arrives at a state of perfection in this life.

MAN IS MULTIFACETED

There are many aspects to man's nature and many ways of categorizing these facets. Basically, man is material (body) and immaterial (soul). Within his body are many material functions. The function of seeing is not the same as hearing; the nervous system is different, separate and yet related to seeing and hearing. These are distinct yet related functions of the material part of man.

Likewise the immaterial aspect of man's being has different yet related functions. Soul, spirit, heart, mind, will, conscience are all facets of man's immaterial nature, and it is often difficult to draw hard and fast distinctions between them. For instance, the soul is that with which we love God (Matt. 22:37); it is that which wars again the flesh (I Peter 2:11). It can magnify the Lord as can the spirit (Luke 1:46-47). And yet the spirit can partake of corruption (II Cor. 7:1). If one studies the functions of the heart of man (the nonmaterial concept of heart, that is), he finds that this facet of man often incorporates things which are also attributed to soul, spirit and mind. The point simply is that man viewed as either a material or an immaterial being is multifaceted. Although the study of these various functions and aspects of man (soul, spirit, heart, etc.) is exceedingly profitable, it is not to our point at this juncture. Therefore, we must reserve any detailed discussion for later chapters. As far as forming our basic ideas concerning spirituality is concerned, the multifaceted concept of man alerts us to the fact that the spiritual life will be related to and will affect all these various aspects of man's nature. The "formula for victory" will not be a simple one working only through, for instance, the spirit. It will undoubtedly have to involve the heart, mind, conscience, and so forth.

MAN IS A UNITY

Although man is a many-faceted being, and even though these facets of man participate in the conflict between the old and new natures when a person becomes a believer, still man is a unity and acts as one. What I do, *I* do, not a part of myself. It is a mistake to speak of "my old nature doing thus and so" or to say that "this stemmed from the soul and not the spirit." True, cer-

tain aspects of my being may originate an action, but that action is performed by me, not part of me. Too often when we speak like that, we tend to excuse ourselves from some evil action by relegating it to some part of our being which somehow becomes detached so that we are relieved of responsibility.

Galatians 2:20 is used frequently to support this kind of idea. The impression is given that Christ does it all almost apart from me. I am supposed to retire and then Christ will live out His life in me so that I am assured of spiritual victory if only I can keep out of the way enough. But the verse says not only that *Christ* lives in me but that Christ lives in *me,* and the life is a life which *I* live—to be sure by faith—but nevertheless I live it. Whatever is done, whether for good or for evil, I do, for there is no other way for the old nature, the new nature, the soul, the spirit, or any other aspect of my being to express itself than through me. Therefore, I am responsible for my actions and cannot shift the blame to some part of me which I have tried to make not a part of me. The hand that pulls the trigger to murder brings imprisonment or death to the whole person; the eye that lusts brings disease to the whole body that committed fornication; the mind that rationalized its way out of the will of God affects the whole life; the heart that set its affection on the wrong object shapes the effort of the whole person. No one can say that it was merely the hand or the eye or the mind or the heart that is to blame. The person is to blame.

Conversely, by the grace of God, when through His power and ability something good is done, He recognizes that I did it and rewards the person for it. Even though the action stems from the new nature or the renewed mind, and although it is His power which enables the act to be performed, still I do it, and the Lord acknowledges that by giving me a reward. Otherwise, if He does it all apart from me or through a completely passive me, then He ought simply to reward Himself at the judgment. But this is not the case, and it is simply because the many aspects of man form a united person.

These, then, are some of the basic characteristics of man which are pertinent to the spiritual life. Some of these require further discussion, but it is only necessary at this point to lay a foundation of these ideas in the thinking of the reader.

4

THE OLD AND THE NEW

THE MOMENT ONE ACCEPTS Jesus Christ as his personal Saviour he becomes a new creation (II Cor. 5:17). The life of God within him begets a new nature which remains with him along with the old as long as he lives. Understanding the presence, position and relationship of the old and new within the life of a believer is essential to experiencing a wholesome and balanced spiritual life.

We have already seen that everyone born into this world is a sinner because of the sin nature with which he is born. We are *by nature,* the apostle says, children of wrath, and this nature produces all kinds of sinful acts (Eph. 2:3). Sometimes the sin nature is referred to as the flesh. Actually the word *flesh* has several meanings. (1) Sometimes it simply means the material body of a person (I Cor. 15:39). (2) Often it indicates people as a whole (Rom. 3:20). (3) But frequently it is used in Scripture to indicate the sin nature (Rom. 7:18). What does it mean when used in this way? To answer this question it is necessary to find a satisfactory definition of the word *nature.* Too often when people think of the sin nature and the new nature they picture two distinct people who live inside their bodies. One is a grisly, horrifying, degenerate man while the other is a handsome, young, victorious-looking man. Representations like this are not necessarily to be discarded entirely though they often lead to the idea that it is not really I who do these things but that "little man" inside me. In other words, they often lead to a false disjuncture in the individual personality.

It is far better to define nature in terms of a capacity. Thus the old nature of the flesh is that capacity which all men have to serve and please self. Or one might say that it is the capacity to

leave God out of one's life. It would not be inclusive enough to define the sin nature in terms of a capacity to do evil, because it is more than that. There are many things which are not necessarily in themselves evil but which stem from the old nature. They simply are things which leave God out. The flesh, then, is that old capacity which all men have to live lives which exclude God. In the Christian the flesh is that same capacity to leave God out of his life and actions.

The sin nature is also called the old man (Rom. 6:6; Col. 3:9). This phrase seems to emphasize the source of the capacity to glorify self instead of God; that is, it takes us back to Adam from whom we all received our sin natures.

Conversion brings with it a new capacity with which we may now serve God and righteousness. Before salvation we were servants of sin, but now we may be servants of righteousness (Rom. 6:18-20). The unsaved man has only one capacity, but the Christian has two. This means that the unsaved person has only one course of action—to serve sin and self, or to leave God out of his life—while the believer has an option. He may serve God, and as long as he is in a human body he may also choose to leave God out and live according to the old nature.

The new nature comes from God Himself (II Peter 1:4). Paul calls it the new man in contrast to the old man: "That ye put off concerning the former conversation the old man, which is corrupt according to the deceitful lusts; and be renewed in the spirit of your mind; and that ye put on the new man, which after God is created in righteousness and true holiness" (Eph. 4:22-25). There is a very close relationship between the new nature and the power of the Holy Spirit (Gal. 5:25), and there is constant conflict between the two capacities (Gal. 5:17; Rom. 7:15-25; 8:6).

These two capacities are not like two reels of tape on which are stored separate sets of actions which can be printed out on a computer. Actually, the same action might belong to either nature. Recreation, for instance, is not an evil thing. And yet it might be engaged in as an evidence of the old capacity when it leaves God out; and it may on another occasion be a very important part of one's spiritual life. What distinguishes the old from the new is not necessarily the action itself but the use of it. So both reels of tape may have a number of actions on them

which are exactly the same. Indeed, probably the majority of things we do in daily living could be from either capacity and therefore in the illustration appear on both tapes; but it is I in pushing the button on each action who determines from which tape it comes. And it is I, not half of me, who performs the action; for I, as the computer, print out the action in daily life. Recognizing this dual capacity in every single believer, it is also important to understand that each facet of the Christian's personality can be involved in actions which stem from the old and the new.

The Mind

The words used in the Old and New Testaments for *mind* express a variety of ideas. The Bible has no word for brain; therefore, the concept of mind does not mean the physical organ but the varied functions of intellect, volition and emotions which are associated with mind in the Scriptures. These ideas include the ability to think or apprehend, to judge, feel, determine; to think critically; the process of comprehending so as to arrive at a result. The mind itself seems to be neutral, its moral quality being determined by the old or new capacity to which it is subjected.

The mind of the unsaved person is not described in very flattering terms in the Scriptures. It is evil (Gen. 6:5); it is reprobate (Rom. 1:28). This is due to the rejection of the light of revelation which God gives to all men in nature (Rom. 1:18-21). In other words, it is self-determined reprobation brought on by man's willful rejection of what he could know of the power of God through the universal revelation of God in the creation. The unsaved man because of the fall is without a critical faculty (Rom. 3:11) when it comes to understanding the things of God. This is not to say that he is without understanding or intelligence, but it is to say that his mind is darkened and vain (Eph. 4:17-18). Actually it is at war with God (Rom. 8:6-7). It is defiled (literally, dyed with another color, Titus 1:15) and corrupt (I Tim. 6:5). All of this is due to the fact that Satan has blinded the mind of the unregenerate person "lest the light of the glorious gospel of Christ, who is the image of God, should shine unto them" (II Cor. 4:4). This is a very crucial verse to remember in the matter of witnessing, for it reminds us that getting a person saved involves

more than convincing him of the truth of the gospel. You may argue, persuade, convince and bring someone to the point of agreement, but unless there is a removal of that satanic blindness there will be no conversion. And, of course, no human being is powerful enough to remove such blindness—only God the Holy Spirit can do that. Intellectual arguments have their rightful place—and I am certainly not pleading for an unintelligent presentation of the gospel—but they must be presented in the power of the Spirit before they can be effective unto salvation.

These biblical characteristics of the unsaved person's mind do not mean that he is incapable of good thinking or right action. In His graciousness to man, God has bestowed some very marvelous minds on mankind which they have used for the common good. These are gifts of His common grace. All of us are indebted to many unsaved people for the advances which their minds have given to our contemporary civilization. And yet with all of the qualities which men's minds may possess, they are still afflicted with the undesirable characteristics described in the Scriptures, although these characteristics may not be so evident in one person as in another. And they are not evident in every area of thought and life. But they are particularly seen when the unsaved person tries to apply his natural mind to the sphere of religion; and that in turn, of course, affects to a certain degree his whole viewpoint on life.

Furthermore, it should be remembered that the Christian may choose to allow these characteristics of the old mind to show themselves in his life. God has judged the old capacity with its directive principle so that we need not be controlled by it, but it is not yet extinct and we can be controlled by it. If allowed to exercise itself, it can manifest itself as the evil, reprobate, carnal, uncritical, darkened, vain, defiled, corrupt and blinded mind that it is.

With the miracle of regeneration comes the mind of Christ (I Cor. 2:16). What is the mind of Christ? It is above all else the attitude of not thinking of ourselves more highly than we ought, and this is the frame of mind which we must cultivate (Phil. 2:5). Here again is an example of the need for balance in spiritual living as it relates to the mind. We have the mind of Christ and yet we are obliged to think (an active voice imperative

in Phil. 2:5 translated passively as "let" in the A.V.) humbly. God
has done something and we are to do something in order to reveal
what He has done. Divine and human works are both involved.
But what is this which we are to think? In accordance with the
perfect example of Christ, we are to think in complete submission to the will of God.

In order to have the mind of Christ, submission to the will of
God, we will have to understand what the will of God is, and
that requires thinking (Eph. 5:17). If discerning His will happens to involve the area of doubtful things in Christian conduct,
we shall have to use the mind in arriving at a conclusion (Rom.
14:5). The Holy Spirit's ministry of teaching our understandings
will be requisite (John 16:13; cf. Luke 24:45). Furthermore, we
shall have to gird the mind (I Peter 1:13) so that we do not have
loose, undisciplined thoughts; girding necessitates capturing the
mind (II Cor. 10:5). How important these responsibilities are in
these days especially. There is so much loose thinking (if there
is any thinking done at all!). People run on emotions rather
than intellect in the Christian life, and instead of leading their
thoughts captive unto the obedience of Christ, every billboard
and each TV commercial leads them captive to the obedience of
lust. Our minds ought to be giving the stimulation of Christianity
to the world; instead the stimuli of the world govern our minds.

What is the way to practice the mind of Christ? Is there a "secret" for victory in this area? Yes, there is, and it is no secret!
The formula is a continuous renewing of the mind (Rom. 12:2).
Notice that this is a complete metamorphosis, not a surface
change. And notice too that the verb in this verse is in the present tense, indicating that it is a continuous process. This reminds
us again of the fact that spirituality is not an instantaneous
achievement but one that requires time for maturity. In Romans
12:2 Paul states the negative of being transformed by the renewing of the mind in the phrase "be not conformed to this world."
That word *conformed* appears also in I Peter 1:14, and might
be translated in Romans 12:2 "Be not fashioned according to
this world." The picture is of putting the cheap veneer of the
world over the genuine life of a believer. Usually veneer is a
more expensive material placed over inexpensive wood, but in
this verse the image is reversed. The world is the cheap veneer

which too often is placed over the expensive work of regeneration, and Paul says this ought not to be. This means that thoughts, ideas, standards, ambitions, conceptions must all be those which conform to the will of God, and we must be constantly renewing our minds along these lines in order to exhibit the mind of Christ.

There is also another aspect to this formula for victory in relation to the mind, and that is Paul's doctrine of "The Power of Positive Thinking" as found in Philippians 4:8: "Finally, brethren, whatsoever things are true, whatosever things are honest [worthy of reverence or honorable], whatsoever things are just [righteous in God's sight—and how this cuts across the standards of the world today], whatsoever things are pure [separated unto God like the Nazarite was], whatsoever things are lovely [admirable so that you are motivated to do the same yourself], whatsoever things are of good report [winsome]; if there be any virtue, and if there be any praise, think on these things." We are responsible for considering these things in a world which is filled with all the opposite and in conflict with an old mind which constantly wars within us. Luther is reported to have said, "You cannot prevent a bird flying over your head but you can prevent his making a nest in your hair." Continual renewing of the basic ideas of the mind (Rom. 12:2) and persistent concentration on right thoughts (Phil. 4:8) are the secret for effectively manifesting the mind of Christ in the daily life. This is the characteristic of genuine spirituality.

THE HEART

Of all the words that speak of some aspect of the immaterial part of man (including soul and spirit), the word *heart* is the broadest in meaning and the most frequently used. Only twice does it seem to be used of the seat of physical life (II Sam. 18: 14; II Kings 9:24); in all the other more than seven hundred occurrences it relates to some aspect of the immaterial nature of man.

1. The heart is the seat of our intellectual life and as such is a synonym for mind. The heart has thoughts (Heb. 4:12) and evil thoughts proceed from it (Matt. 15:19). And yet it is the place in which we should hide our knowledge of the Word of God (Ps. 119:11).

2. The heart is also the seat of our emotional life. This is the usage that most would think of first when considering the meaning of heart. The heart loves (Deut. 6:5), rejoices (Ps. 104:15), sorrows (Rom. 9:2), desires (Ps. 37:4) and expresses many other emotions.

3. The heart can also will. Purposing or willing is related to the heart (II Cor. 9:7). The heart chooses (Exodus 7:23), it can be turned aside (Exodus 14:5), it seeks (Deut. 4:29), and it can be hardened (Heb. 4:7).

4. Sometimes the word *heart* is used metaphorically for the middle or inner part of something. The Scriptures speak of the heart of the sea (Exodus 15:8), the heart of heaven (Deut. 4:11) and the heart of the earth (Matt. 12:40). This usage has no bearing on the spiritual life.

5. Our principal interest in the use of the word *heart* is in relation to the spiritual life, but first we need to notice how the old and new capacities may affect the heart.

The heart of the unsaved man is characterized in rather severe terms. This means that the intellectual, emotional, volitional and spiritual aspects of his life are all affected in these ways. His heart is called hard and impenitent (Rom. 2:5). The word *hard* means calloused or insensitive to spiritual things. It is also impenitent or unrepentant which would naturally follow from being insensitive. It is blinded (Eph. 4:18), it is evil (Jer. 3:17), and it is uncircumcised (Acts 7:51). It can be deceived (James 1:26) and it can deceive (Jer. 17:9). It can also sink to the perverted state of being without natural affection (Rom. 1:31).

Salvation brings into the life a new capacity and with it a new ability to think right, to love God, to purpose to do the will of God, to have a changed heart. The heart of the Christian (and this means his intellectual, emotional, volitional and spiritual life) can now be true and pure (Heb. 10:22). It is now circumcised (Rom. 2:29); that is, it has put off the sinful flesh. Now the heart can become a vital center of spiritual living for the believer.

With the heart a person believes unto righteousness (Rom. 10:10), and with the right kind of heart the righteous man can live the Christian life. The heart is the abode of the indwelling Christ (Eph. 3:17) and Holy Spirit (II Cor. 1:22). The heart is the center of obedience in the many aspects of Christian living (Rom.

6:17). It is with the heart that we love God (Matt. 22:37) and in the heart the love of God is shed abroad (Rom. 5:5). It may be said, then, that the indwelling Christ and Spirit affect all of the aspects of our being (for heart includes them all), and we in turn are to love and obey God with all the facets of our nature (that is, with all our heart).

But this does not happen apart from the exercise of responsible human action. We are severely warned that a believer's heart may become hardened, that is, calloused or insensitive to spiritual things (Heb. 3:8, 13). Sin is deceitful and it can lure one into the position where he does not respond to the promptings of the Lord and His Spirit even though they continue to indwell the heart. The deceitfulness of sin forms a callous over the heart which obscures the manifestation of the indwelling Godhead. In the Hebrews passage are listed three preventives for a calloused Christian heart. The first is daily exhortation of one another (3:13). An isolated Christian may become a calloused Christian, for he needs the encouragement and watchful concern of other believers. The second is the Word of God used in the life to affect all its parts (notice that soul, spirit, body and heart are all mentioned in Heb. 4:12). The verse does not teach that the Word of God divides between soul and spirit as if to cut off the soulish part of our being and leave the spiritual. If it taught that, then it would also teach that the marrow is cut off and the joints are left! It states that the Word divides or cuts right through to the innermost parts of man, both immaterial (soul and spirit) and material (joints and marrow). In other words, the Word lays bare all parts of us to expose every aspect of our being to its teachings. Of course, a life that allows this to take place will never have a calloused heart.

The third preventive for callousness is the life of prayer (Heb. 4:14-16). When help is needed as it so often is, we find it at the throne of grace. But we must come. The tenses of the verbs in these verses do not indicate an ever flowing supply of grace but bursts of grace, so to speak, that are given each time we come. Thus our responsibility to come is emphasized; otherwise, we will not experience the grace that is available. These three— fellowship, the Word and prayer—will enable the believer to ex-

perience the new life in his heart: in his intellect, emotions, will
and spiritual life.

THE CONSCIENCE

Conscience in man is that faculty by which he distinguishes
between that which is morally right and wrong. It is interesting
that in the Old Testament where the word does not appear at all
the idea is expressed by the term *heart* (II Sam. 24:10; Job 27:
6), showing once again that the concept of the heart is the largest one as far as the facets of the immaterial part of man are
concerned.

All men have a conscience (Rom. 2:15) and it can be a right
guide (John 8:9). It may also only seem to be right when actually it is leading the person down the wrong road (Acts 23:1).
Thus in salvation we need to be cleansed from an evil conscience
(Heb. 10:22), for even in practice the conscience has ceased to
function properly and has become defiled (Titus 1:15) and
seared (I Tim. 4:2).

The cleansed conscience of a believer should be put to use in
living the Christian life. It is rather amazing how many broad
spheres of life the conscience is supposed to affect for the spiritual Christian. The Christian's obedience to the laws of his
country is based on heeding the voice of his conscience (Rom.
13:5). It is unfortunate that most of the discussions of this
passage focus on the Christian's responsibility to his country in
war. They ought to emphasize the more prosaic matter of driving
one's car according to a Christian conscience!

Doing a good job for an unworthy employer is also a matter
of conscience for the spiritual believer (I Peter 2:19). It is not
right for a Christian to waste or misuse his employer's time in
the name of "doing something for the Lord." Our consciences
should be able to attest to the quality of the testimony we are
bearing for the Lord (II Cor. 1:12), and the consciences of
others to whom we minister should agree that ours is a proper
testimony (II Cor. 4:2). Have you ever met a Christian who
feels he has no responsibility to any other Christian and who
excuses his lack of concern on the basis of his direct line to heaven
which bypasses all other people, their consciences and even his
own? When Paul wished to call a witness to attest to the truth

of something he was saying, he called on his conscience in the Holy Spirit (Rom. 9:1).

One of the most important and complex aspects of a Christian's life is his social activities, and these, too, should be governed by conscience. In this case it is the conscience of the weaker, more restricted brother which must be considered as a governor on the life of the stronger brother (I Cor. 8:7, 10, 12). This is a difficult principle to practice but one which will be used by the mature, spiritual Christian.

Thus the conscience, though it may lead the unsaved man aright in some areas, cannot save him, since it is defiled, seared and evil. But in regeneration it is cleansed and used by the Lord to guide the believer in his political, vocational, spiritual and social relations.

SOUL AND SPIRIT

The concepts involved in soul and spirit are quite complex and not easily delineated. One scarcely ever finds the words defined, and if so, with a definition that gives little or no help. Here is one: "Soul in man is the subject of personal life, whereof spirit is the principle." Actually, for our purposes we need only to make a few observations about soul and spirit.

1. Every man has a spirit. One needs to affirm this fact because occasionally one finds someone who teaches that until one is saved he has no spirit and after conversion it is the spirit (Spirit) that is the sole cause of the spiritual life. That all men are born with a spirit is quite clearly taught in the Bible. Notice James 2:26: "For as the body without the spirit is dead, so faith without works is dead also." In other words, a man in order to be a living person has to have a spirit; without it, he is dead. First Corinthians 2:11 also states clearly that all men have a spirit and it is this that gives them sympathetic understanding of each other. The human spirit is a facet of human personality; the Holy Spirit who comes to indwell the believer at conversion is a Person. He works through the human spirit (Acts 13:4), but He is not the spirit which is in man.

2. The difference between soul and spirit (when used in relation to the immaterial part of man) is not one of material substance but one of function (and even these functional differences

are not always too clear). But soul and spirit are both immaterial. There are really only two substance categories in the world—material and immaterial, and both soul and spirit belong to the immaterial. Therefore, when speaking of man's makeup as far as substance is concerned, one must conclude that his makeup is twofold—material and immaterial (simply because there is no possible third category). But when describing man's functions, it is obvious that his functional makeup is quite varied. In the material part of his being his many functions include seeing, hearing, a nervous system, etc. In the immaterial part of his being his many functions are expressed through heart, mind, conscience, soul, spirit, will, etc. Sometimes these functions overlap and sometimes they are distinct.

3. The functions of soul and spirit are often similar and sometimes distinct. Soul and spirit can both glorify God (Luke 1:46-47). Soul and spirit were both involved in the sacrifice of Christ (John 10:15; 19:30). Yet the Holy Spirit seems to work through the spirit, not the soul (Rom. 8:16), and when the basic words become adjectives, quite a contrast develops. The soulish man is the unsaved person (I Cor. 2:14; cf. Jude 19) while the spiritual man is one whose life is properly related to God. In I Corinthians 15:44 the soulish body is the present unresurrected body, while the spiritual body is suited to the resurrection experience. Therefore, one may say that sometimes the concepts differ in that soulishness seems to be related to this world while spirituality is related to God.

4. But this distinction must not be carried over into the present spiritual life so as to teach, as some do, that anything that has to do with the soul is automatically carnal while anything that concerns the spirit is guaranteed to promote spirituality. Both soul and spirit can promote the spiritual life of the believer, and both can be hindrances. The soul must love God (Matt. 22:37), and it stands against the lusts of the flesh (I Peter 2:11). The spirit witnesses to give assurance (Rom. 8:16), and the singing and sacrifices of the believer are to be spiritual (Col. 3:16; I Peter 2:5). Both soul and spirit may further the spiritual life. But both may hinder if not properly aligned and controlled. The spirit of the believer can partake of corruption (II Cor. 7:1), and the soul of the Christian needs watching (Heb. 13:17). Both need

to be laid bare by the Word of God (Heb. 4:12), and regardless how one interprets the teaching of I Thessalonians 5:23 about the makeup of man ("I pray God your whole spirit and soul and body be preserved blameless"), it certainly declares that both soul and spirit need to be included in the process of daily sanctification. Neither of these verses teaches that soul is to be avoided and spirit is to be cultivated as the way to spiritual victory.

Thus we observe that the concepts involved in soul and spirit are complex, and yet it is clear that both have their proper function in promoting the spiritual life. One writer has summed up the difficulties in these words well: "There are few words more vaguely used by devout persons, or which present greater difficulties to the learned, or open wider fields of speculation for the thoughtful."[1]

THE WILL

Actually the Bible expresses much more interest in discussing the will of God than it does in considering the will of man. And when it deals with man's will it does so in a very unsystematic fashion. Furthermore, the distinction between an old and new will is not linked to the word itself but is related to the two capacities within a believer. With the word *mind* we saw a fairly sharp distinction between the unregenerated mind and the mind of Christ. But with the concept of will, the distinction between old and new is stated more in terms of what *I* do, or what my will wills either the old or new capacity to do.

Here are a few interesting uses of the concept of will in the Scriptures. For one thing an unsaved man may will a good thing as the centurion did when he was "willing to save Paul" and commanded that the prisoners aboard ship should not be killed (Acts 27:43). Just as the conscience of an unbeliever may lead him aright, so he may will to do a good thing. The believer with his capacities to do the will of God or his own will may will a right matter (Titus 3:8) or wrong actions (I Tim. 6:9; James 4:4).

These two capacities which express themselves according to the way a believer wills are sharply seen in Romans 7:15-25. There are certain facts about this section that are often not clear.

1. E. G. Ounchard, "The Epistle of St. James," *A Bible Commentary for English Readers,* ed. Charles John Ellicott, VIII, 361.

For one thing the experience of a believer is in view; otherwise Paul could not say "I delight in the law of God" (v. 22). For another thing this passage certainly demonstrates that human nature (even that of the believer) is not essentially good (v. 18). Too, the intensity of the expressions in the paragraph show that this was Paul's own experience.

What is the apostle saying in this section? Many, teaching on the victorious life, assert that Paul in Romans 7 was living in weakness, carnality and immaturity and that he did not know the secret of victory until he came out into the light of chapter 8. Therefore, they conclude, we must leave Romans 7 and get into Romans 8. The writer cannot agree with this viewpoint because it would not properly interpret phrases like "sin that dwells in me" (v. 17; what happened to it when he got into Romans 8?) or "I delight in the law of God" (v. 22; that kind of expression should not come until chapter 8 according to this viewpoint). Furthermore, chapter 7 (if we are to make anything of the order of these chapters) comes *after* chapter 6 in which Paul has already given the secret of victory. What Paul is saying in 7:15-25 is twofold: First, he is saying that all believers have these two capacities within their being—the capacity to serve sin and the capacity to delight in the law of God. And these two capacities remain with the Christian as long as he lives. Second, he also confesses that in the constant warfare between the two natures his old nature occasionally erupts. Notice that he says that sometimes he does the evil that he does not wish to do (v. 19). In other words, the two capacities within his being were in constant conflict, and even the Apostle Paul did not always live in constant victory over the old nature. Lest anyone think that later on he accomplished this victorious life, remember his own testimony to still being the chief of sinners at the close of his life (I Tim. 1:15). The Christian does not have to live in defeat, but he does have to live all his life with the sin nature. God has provided the way of victory, but because God has also given us a will we may choose not to use that provision. And, too, because God has not made the flesh any better in the believer, because it has not been refined, it is a powerful enemy with which we have to live.

This brings to mind another question: Is the will free? A lot

has been written about the "free will of man" and the sovereignty of God. In a certain sense man's will is free to make choices. In I Corinthians 7 several times Paul says that the will may choose among several correct possibilities so that any choice would be correct (vv. 36, 37, 39). All of the appeals of the Bible to man's will clearly imply that man has the real possibility of responsible choice. And yet it is true that no man has an entirely free will. It is governed and restricted in many ways simply by the limitations of being human. We are not free to live for months without food and water. We cannot will to live without sleep. Further, we are limited by circumstances. We cannot will to be in more than one place at a time. And, too, we are limited by God's purposes in this world. This does not mean that God rules as a dictator, but it does mean that He is the supreme Ruler of the universe who designed its operation so as to glorify Himself. Perhaps the best way to express in a balanced way these two ideas (that man seems to have certain freedom of choice and at the same time God is in complete control) would be to say that God has given man genuine responsibility with regard to his actions and in the discharge of this responsibility he makes real choices.

The practical point concerning this with regard to the spiritual life is simply that what I do I have willed to do and am therefore responsible for. It is not some thing or entity or "little man" inside me who does these things I do not want to do; I do them. My will makes the choice and is responsible for the action. I am responsible and accountable. Have you noticed in this entire discussion of all these aspects of the immaterial part of man that the Bible does not present a picture of two of everything inside a person? There are two capacities but these express themselves through a single mind, a single heart, a single conscience, a single soul, a single spirit, a single will. The two capacities of a believer express themselves through the many single facets of the individual person. And it seems that it is the will that activates either the old or new capacity.

The present trend in psychology is away from the notion of will as a faculty and toward the viewpoint that it is an expression of the total self or personality. Normal life includes the capacity for making decisions, and one is re-

sponsible for his choices. That choice which makes all
others the more meaningful is commitment to Christ.[2]

And that commitment is by an act of the will in a responsible
response to the appeal of God. "I beseech you . . . that ye present your bodies" (Rom. 12:1). How intricate must be the details
of the plan of God who can govern all things, allow human choice,
and yet get glory to Himself through people who are permitted
to make choices between the old and the new.

2. Everett F. Harrison, "Will," *Baker's Dictionary of Theology,* p. 552.

5

UNITED WITH CHRIST

PROBABLY the most important doctrinal fact underpinning the spiritual life is the believer's union with Christ. It is foundational to the truth of cocrucifixion of the Christian with Christ, which in turn is the basis for freedom from the power of sin. Unfortunately, this concept is little understood, unbalanced in its presentation, and unused in application.

THE CONCEPT

The concept of being united with Christ is developed chiefly by Paul in his use and explanation of the phrase "in Christ." Our Lord announced the idea in the upper room before His crucifixion when He declared, "At that day ye shall know that I am in my Father, and ye in me, and I in you" (John 14:20). He also illustrated this relationship when He spoke of the branches being in the vine (John 15:4). But the Apostle Paul gave us the far-reaching revelation of the meaning of this concept.

He uses the idea in relation to our heavenly calling (Phil. 3:14), election in Christ (Eph. 1:4), forgiveness (Eph. 1:7; 4:32; Col. 1:14), redemption (Rom. 3:24), freedom from condemnation (Rom. 8:1), freedom from the law (Gal. 2:4), justification (Gal. 2:17) and life (Rom. 6:11, 23; 8:2). In other words, our justification, or salvation, is vitally related to being "in Christ." Too, our future bodily resurrection is guaranteed by being "in Christ" (I Cor. 15:22). But our principal interest in the concept is its relation to our present sanctification or to the Christian life. Paul taught that in Christ believers are sanctified (I Cor. 1:2), rooted and built up (Col. 2:7), taught (Eph. 4:21), guarded (Phil. 4:7), led in triumph (II Cor. 2:14), and have boldness

49

and access to God (Eph. 3:12). It is easy to see that many of the vital activities of Christian living are based on our position in Christ.

What does this concept mean? My own definition is simply this: to be in Christ is the redeemed man's new environment in the sphere of resurrection life. The key word is *environment*, for being in Christ is not a barren state or an almost unreal positional truth (as it is often presented), but a vital, pulsating, functioning involvement. The chief characteristic of this environment is resurrection life, the life of Christ Himself. Another writer speaking of this same position of the believer describes it this way: "He has been transplanted into a new soil and a new climate, and both soil and climate are Christ."[1]

In trying to define or describe a difficult concept like this one, it often helps to look at the opposite. What is the opposite of being in Christ? It is being in Adam and encompassed by the environment of death (I Cor. 15:22). This is a position which all men have by birth, for all sinned in Adam (Rom. 5:12). Notice the contrast in each area—justification, sanctification, glorification—between being in Adam and being in Christ.

Area	In Adam	In Christ
Justification	None (condemnation)	Complete (eternal life)
Sanctification	Slaves to sin	Servants of righteousness
Glorification	The second death	Resurrection unto life

Thus in relation to sanctification or the Christian life, which is our chief interest in this book, being in Christ frees us from the bondage of sin and enables us to live righteously before God. However, before seeing how this works out, it is necessary to consider one other question: How did we achieve this position? How is it that we are placed in Christ?

1. J. S. Stewart, *A Man in Christ,* p. 157.

THE MEANS

The answer to this question: We are placed in Christ not by anything we can do, but by the sovereign baptizing work of the Holy Spirit. "For by one Spirit are we all baptized into one body, whether we be Jews or Gentiles, whether we be bond or free; and have been made to drink into one Spirit (I Cor. 12:13). In other words, this position which is the basis for all victorious living is effected by something God does for us through the baptizing work of the Holy Spirit.

There is probably no work of the Holy Spirit which is more confused than this one. Many who have had some climactic spiritual experience subsequent to salvation have chosen to label it "the baptism of the Spirit." And they have become so wrapped up in a precious experience that they find it difficult to comprehend the biblical doctrine. This has tragic ramifications, for a lack of understanding of the doctrine of the baptizing work of the Holy Spirit will obscure the important truth of union with Christ which is the basis for genuine spirituality.

There are at least four characteristics of the baptizing work of the Spirit:

1. All believers have been baptized by the Spirit. This ministry is not reserved for a select few. If that were so, the body of Christ would be composed only of those selected or spiritually qualified to be baptized. In the key passage (I Cor. 12:13) notice that Paul did not say that only the spiritual people at Corinth had been baptized. He said *all*. Notice too that he did not exhort them to be baptized as some groups do today in order to become spiritual. Certainly this would have been an easy solution to the problems generated by the carnality in the church at Corinth, if it were a valid solution. But baptism, in and of itself, does not give power; it sets up a relationship which in turn can unleash power. Further evidence that all believers have been baptized is apparent in the lack of exhortations or commands to be baptized by the Spirit anywhere in the New Testament. If some Christians have been baptized and some have not, surely there would be somewhere an exhortation to those who had not been. But nowhere is there such, which simply confirms the fact that all believers have experienced this work of the Spirit.

2. Each believer is baptized by the Spirit only once; baptism is not repeated. Each believer is baptized at the time of his conversion, and there is no scriptural reference which would indicate that the same person is baptized a second time. Indeed, the Greek tense of the word *baptize* in I Corinthians 12:13 indicates an unrepeated experience. Think for a moment of the implications of repeated baptisms. Since Spirit baptism places a person in the body of Christ, a second baptism would mean that that person had been removed from the body since his first baptism and was on the occasion of the second being reinstated into the body. Such an idea is completely foreign to Scripture.

3. Each believer is baptized once, and all believers have been baptized whether they know it or not. This which God does for us occurs whether or not we are conscious of it. I do not mean to imply that no experience results from this new position, but the baptism itself, the actual placing of the believer in the body of Christ, is something which happens whether or not we have any experience or consciousness or understanding of it.

4. The fact that all believers are baptized into the body does not in itself guarantee that power will be experienced or displayed in the life. The Corinthians, all of whom had been baptized, fell far short of displaying the power of God in their lives. They were baptized and carnal. The Galatians too had been baptized but were far from spiritual Christians (Gal. 3:27; cf. 1:6; 4:9). The demonstration of power compatible with our new position involves other factors, but the position itself can be attained in no other way than by the baptizing work of the Spirit.

Thus union with Christ means the introduction of the believer into that new environment of Christ's resurrection life by means of the baptizing work of the Holy Spirit. Formerly in Adam, we are now in Christ, transferred by a miracle of God's grace.

When I was a student the transplanting of the cornea of the eye was a new and startling operation. One particular case gained a great deal of publicity, for it involved transplantation of the cornea of a condemned criminal awaiting execution into the eye of a blind citizen of that state. The prospective recipient visited the donor before his execution, and this of course received even more publicity in the papers. In due time the execution was carried out, the operation was performed and the sightless man was

able to see. That cornea illustrates very well what is true of every believer in Christ. Formerly he was, as the eye in that criminal, in Adam—condemned justly to death. There was no hope of escape apart from a miraculous intervention. And that is exactly what happened when he believed in Christ. A miracle did occur and he was removed from the condemnation of death in Adam and placed through the baptizing work of the Spirit into Christ. And then that one who was condemned was justified and placed in that new sphere of resurrection life with all of its privileges and responsibilities. This is the true story of every believer in Christ.

THE CONSEQUENCES

If union with Christ involves (as it does) partaking of all that He is, then the most important consequence of this union as far as the victorious life is concerned is that it is the means of actualizing our cocrucifixion with Him (Col. 2:12; note especially Rom. 6:1-10). Being associated with Christ by baptism into His death, burial and resurrection is the basis for the crucifixion of the believer's sin nature and his victory over sin; and this is all based on our union with Him which has been accomplished for us by the baptizing work of the Spirit.

Some become so concerned with the question of whether or not water baptism is in Romans 6 that they miss the principal point of the passage. One extreme wants to be certain that water baptism is taught there in order to justify immersion as the mode of baptism; the other extreme seeks to eliminate water entirely from the passage in order to avoid the conclusion that immersion is the proper form of the ordinance. Certain facts seem to be obvious. (1) Water baptism by whatever mode or all of them together could never accomplish what is said to have been accomplished in the passage. Water cannot crucify the old man and provide the basis for not serving sin (v. 6). (2) On the other hand, it is not easy to remove the imagery of immersion from these verses. Baptism in relation to death, burial and resurrection is an obvious picture of immersion. The proper resolution of the matter is to admit that although it is the baptism of the Spirit which does the work, it is water baptism which pictures what is done. Water

baptism is the object in this object lesson, but the work of the Spirit is what makes the lesson true.

What is it that has happened? A death has occurred for believers because of the union with Christ in His death. What is death? Some views of the victorious life are forced to define death as extinction since they teach that the sin nature, being dead, is eradicated. Others, more moderate, would have to consider death as cessation since they teach that, although the sin nature is still present in the believer, he can cease from sinning in this life. Thus death means a cessation of the activities (but not of the presence) of the sin nature. This is probably the impression created by most speakers on this passage. But death does not mean either extinction or cessation; it always means separation. Physical death is the separation of the immaterial part of man from the material body. It does not mean that the person has become extinct or that he has ceased to be or to function. The unbeliever who dies, for instance, is still conscious and active though apart from his physical, earthly body (Luke 16:19-31). Spiritual death is certainly not extinction or inactivity. Every unsaved person walking the face of the earth today is spiritually dead but is at the same time existing and active. However, he is separated from God and this is what makes him spiritually dead. The second death is the eternal state of separation which unbelievers will *experience* in the lake of fire. There could be no such experience if death means extinction or cessation. Death always means separation, and it does in Romans 6 as well.

What, then, is the crucifixion of Romans 6 a separation from? To answer this we need only remind ourselves of the subject of the chapter, "Shall we continue in sin, that grace may abound?" (v. 1). In other words, the death to sin of Romans 6 is a separation from the power of the sin nature to cause the believer to continue in sin. It is separation from the domination of sin over a Christian's life. This is accomplished by the crucifixion of the sin nature in order to "destroy" the body of sin so that we need not serve sin (v. 6). That word *destroy* does not mean to annihilate, which would infer that the sin nature is eradicated in the Christian. Notice its use in II Thessalonians 2:8: "And then shall that Wicked [one] be revealed, whom the Lord shall consume with the spirit of his mouth, and shall destroy with the brightness

of his coming." The man of sin is "destroyed" at the second coming of Christ and yet he continues to exist in the lake of fire into
which the devil is cast a thousand years later (Rev. 20:10; in the
Greek the plural verb "shall be tormented" indicates that all
three beings are alive in the lake of fire forever and ever). Another interesting use of the word is in Luke 13:7: "Then said he
unto the dresser of his vineyard, Behold, these three years I come
seeking fruit on this fig tree, and find none: cut it down; why
cumbereth it the ground?" Here the word is translated "cumbereth." Obviously the fig tree did not destroy the ground in the
sense of annihilating it, but it did make the ground useless or idle
as far as serving a good purpose was concerned. In the same sense
the sin nature has been "destroyed"; that is, it has been made
ineffective, useless, so that we do not have to continue in sin.

The Scripture speaks both of the crucifixion of the old nature
(Rom. 6:6) and the crucifixion of the person (Gal. 2:20). This is
no contradiction; rather it is simply another illustration of the
unity of man's being. Thus what is said of or attributed to one
aspect or facet of man's being may be predicated of him. Although Christ lives in me, it is a life which I live (Gal. 2:20).
Even though apart from Him we can do nothing (John 15:5), we
labor to be accepted of Him (II Cor. 5:9). With the heart man
believes unto righteousness, and I believe. Out of the heart
proceed evil thoughts, and I think evil. The flesh produces hatred,
variance, emulations, wrath, strife (Gal. 5:20), and yet I am the
one who bites and devours others (Gal. 5:15). Thus it is not
strange or out of line for the Scriptures to speak of the crucifixion
of the old nature and of the person.

To recapitulate: Our union with Christ means a separation
from the domination of the sin nature because of its crucifixion.
But it also means a resurrection to newness of living (Rom. 6:4).
Throughout this section of Scripture not only is the death taught
but also our resurrection. The truth includes not only the fact of
separation from the old but also the all-important association with
the new, the risen life of Christ. It is mentioned in every verse
in Romans 6:4-10. Union with Christ, therefore, not only breaks
the power of the old capacity but it also associates us with Him
who gives the power to live according to the new capacity.

When did or does all this happen? Historically, it occurred

when Christ died and rose again. His death and resurrection are
the basis for all these consequences which follow. But as far as
our personal history is concerned this union with Christ does not
happen until we receive the Saviour and at that moment are baptized into His body by the Holy Spirit. The historical actions of
Christ's death and resurrection become part of our personal history when we believe and are baptized into His body. But practically, these truths may be present or absent from our daily experience. The fact that we have been crucified with Christ—that
the power of the sin nature has been broken and made inopera-
tive, that we need not serve sin—this is unalterable and does not
depend on anything I do. But putting this into practice does depend on meeting certain conditions, one of which is reckoning
these things to be true (v. 11). This means counting up the
weight and truth of the facts that have been revealed in verses
1-10 and calculating them to be true *for me*. It has the idea of
considering, evaluating and putting on my own account all that
the crucifixion of Christ means to me in regard to breaking the
power of sin in my life. Failure to make this basic calculation is
often the reason why the practice of these truths may be absent
from the believer's daily experience. What our Lord has done
makes it possible to live the Christian life; putting the possibility
into practice involves a number of other factors, many of which
include the exercise of the human will. We do not choose to make
or break union with Christ; but we may choose whether or not
to enjoy its benefits. We cannot create the new nature nor break
the power of the old; but we can choose to listen to the old and
obey it even after its power has been broken. When one is living
under a dictator of a country he has no choice but to obey the
laws of that dictatorship. If the dictator is overthrown by a
democratic regime and sent into exile in another country, the
citizens are free to live a new kind of life. But it is quite conceivable that there would be some within the country who
would prefer the deposed dictator and seek to serve him even
though his power had been broken. And serve him they could,
receiving their instructions over his clandestine radio and carrying them out while rejecting the freedom into which they had
been brought. The sin nature is like a deposed dictator who was
overthrown by the death of Christ. Christians are citizens of

heaven with a new freedom to live lives pleasing to God. But the sin nature has not been eradicated nor has the individual's will been nullified; therefore it is possible to choose to listen to and follow the promptings of sin, but it will never be possible for sin to regain the domination and control it had before conversion.

PART II

SOME PERSONAL
RESPONSIBILITIES

6

HOW ARE WE SANCTIFIED?

A TITLE LIKE THIS for a single chapter is, of course, a presumption, for it is in reality the question the entire book seeks to answer. But I dare to presume to use it at this point because we need now to survey at least the various persons and things that are involved in the process of sanctification. We have laid some biblical foundations for spirituality; we must turn now to the investigation of our personal responsibilities which are essential to the practice of true spiritual living. In this section we shall look at various specific areas of responsibility, but first we need an answer to the questions What is sanctification? and Who and what sanctifies the Christian?

What is sanctification? The word *sanctify* basically means to set apart. It has the same root as the words *saint* and *holy*. For the Christian, sanctification has three aspects. The first is usually called positional sanctification. This is simply the position every believer enjoys by virtue of being in the family of God by faith in Christ. It involves being set apart as a member of the household of God, and is true regardless of the degree of one's spirituality. To the carnal Corinthians with all of their sinful problems Paul wrote: "But ye are washed, but ye are sanctified, but ye are justified in the name of the Lord Jesus, and by the Spirit of our God" (I Cor. 6:11; the tenses of the Greek verbs indicate an accomplished fact, not something to be attained). Thus there is a sense in which all believers are saints because sanctified (see also I Cor. 1:2; Heb. 10:10).

The second aspect of sanctification is the present experiential or progressive work of continuing to be set apart during the whole of our Christian lives. Every exhortation in the Word to godly living relates to this aspect of sanctification (I Peter 1:16), and this is the area with which biblical spirituality is concerned.

But there is also a sense in which we will not be fully set apart
to God until that day when we see Christ and become as He is
(I John 3:1-3). So there is an aspect to sanctification which is
usually called ultimate sanctification, which awaits our complete
glorification with resurrection bodies (Eph. 5:26-27; Jude 24-25).
Progressive sanctification is the process of maturing in a life that
properly reflects our position, while ultimate sanctification occurs
when our practice and position are in perfect accord.

There is an excellent, though simple, illustration of these three
phases of sanctification. It concerns the little girl who had just
come out of the candy store having spent her allowance on a
lollipop, when she spied her best girl friend coming down the
street toward her. Being a properly brought up child she knew
that unless she could think of something quickly she would be
obliged to offer the lollipop to her little friend. Her dilemma between courtesy and hunger was solved by an action which quickly, certainly, and forever sanctified the lollipop for her own use
alone. And that action was simply to lick it all over on both sides
before her girl friend was alongside. By licking the lollipop she
set it apart for herself; it was not now something the friend
would want. This is like positional sanctification. The moment
we receive the Lord as Saviour, God sets us apart for Himself,
instantaneously, certainly and forever.

But that first lick did not mean much assimilation of the lollipop
for our shrewd little girl. Nevertheless, she took care of that
problem posthaste. She proceeded to keep on licking the candy
and to make it practically what it already was positionally—her
very own. This is progressive sanctification, and it is a process
that continues throughout life. But finally there came that moment when the whole lollipop was completely in her mouth and
stomach, when it was totally possessed by her. So it shall be with
us when we go to be with Christ. We shall then be fully sanctified or fully set apart and possessed by Him. But it is that process
of being made in practice what we are in position and what we
shall be ultimately that is concerned with maturing Christian
life, and it is something which is accomplished by various persons and means. It is an oversimplification to say that God does
it all, and it is a wrong inference to think that He does it apart
from any means.

THE WORK OF GOD IN SANCTIFICATION

Usually speakers on the victorious life emphasize either the work of the indwelling Christ in the believer for sanctification or the ministry of the Holy Spirit. Actually the Scriptures teach that all Persons of the Godhead have a ministry in this regard. In the illustration of the vine and the branches our Lord declared that the Father is the Husbandman who purges the fruitless branch in order that it may bear more fruit (John 15:2). It is the Father to whom the Lord addressed His prayer: "Sanctify them through thy truth: thy word is truth" (John 17:17). The Apostle Paul also asked that "the very God of peace sanctify you wholly" (I Thess. 5:23).

The Son, too, has a major role in the sanctification of the believer. It is Christ who lives within, and through whose power the Christian is enabled to live a life pleasing to God (Gal. 2:20). It is the Lord's purpose to "sanctify and cleanse" the church in order to present her without blemish in the day of His appearing (Eph. 5:26-27; cf. Col. 1:22). The Lord's death is the basis for our positional sanctification (Heb. 13:12; cf. 10:10), and the same Lord is designated in the same epistle as the agent of progressive sanctification (Heb. 2:11; the participle and the verb are both in the present tense in the Greek, indicating continuing action).

And yet to be faithful to the emphasis of Scripture we must observe that the work of the Holy Spirit is given prominence in the process of sanctification. The goal of sanctification is conformity to the image of Christ, and it is the Spirit who changes us "into the same image from glory to glory" (II Cor. 3:18). Through the power of the Spirit we "mortify the deeds of the body" (Rom. 8:13). The Holy Spirit is the Spirit of wisdom and revelation in the knowledge of Christ (Eph. 1:17). The love of God is shed abroad in our hearts by the Spirit (Rom. 5:5). And, of course, the best description of Christlikeness is found in the list of the fruit of the Spirit (Gal. 5:22-23). It is the distinct work of the Spirit who indwells every believer to work in the life effectually and continuously that each might be filled with the fullness of God and walk worthy of the calling with which we are called.

The Work of the Believer in Sanctification

The need for balance is perhaps nowhere greater than in this area. We are so prone to distort emphases, and in this subject we must recognize that although sanctification is the work of God it is also the work of the believer. There is a kind of quietism abroad which rules out any activity on man's part as being "of the flesh." The slogan of this kind of teaching is "Let go and let God." Now, of course, this is a perfectly proper emphasis when it concerns the matter of dedication. We must let go of our own wills, desires, ambitions and let God have His way in our lives. But in the matter of progressive sanctification there is a part that the believer plays which he very definitely must not let go of. Here is a typical statement of such an emphasis:

> The great and glorious fact is this, that, in giving the Holy Ghost, God gave you all you need for all your Christian life and service. It matters not what you are, or what you are not; it matters not what you can do or what you cannot do—you have all in having Him. He has not been given to help you when you do your best; He has been given to do all, because over the very best that you can produce God has written "no good thing." . . . Faith is getting out of the way and letting Him work. Faith is "letting go and letting God." . . . The only "surrender" that He asks of you is the surrender that consents to stop working and lets Him do all.[1]

If this be true then every imperative in the New Testament is a hollow command addressed to the wrong person. But this is not the case, for the Scripture does say very plainly that *I* am to do certain things that are a vital part of the process of sanctification. Otherwise how are we to understand a verse like this: "Having therefore these promises, dearly beloved, let us cleanse ourselves from all filthiness of the flesh and spirit, perfecting holiness in the fear of God" (II Cor. 7:1). And, of course, scores of other references command us to do things which are part of the total process of sanctification. The individual is commanded to do things like "flee from idolatry" (I Cor. 10:14), "flee also youthful lusts, but follow righteousness" (II Tim. 2:22), "meditate upon these things" (I Tim. 4:15), "refuse profane and old wives' fables"

1. David Tryon, *But How,* pp. 16-17.

(I Tim. 4:7), "bear ye one another's burdens" (Gal. 6:2). Of course the person who wants to deemphasize the human agency in sanctification will say that such verses mean that we are to let the Holy Spirit (or the indwelling Christ) do these things through us. But even in verses where the Spirit is mentioned as being involved in carrying out the exhortation, the individual is also included as a necessary part of the process. Notice the careful balance between the individual person and the Spirit in the very basic matter of putting to death the deeds of the body: "But if ye through the Spirit do mortify the deeds of the body, ye shall live" (Rom. 8:13). The subject of the verb "mortify" is "ye" not "Spirit." Nevertheless, what I do I do "through the Spirit." God's working is not suspended because I work; neither is God's working always apart from my working. Again the human and divine are joined in the matter of walking in the Spirit (Gal. 5:16). The life that does not fulfill the lusts of the flesh is the life that walks by means of the Spirit, and yet it is I who am commanded to walk by means of the Spirit. Even Galatians 2:20 reminds me that Christ lives in me *and* I live the life. In other words, it is quite clear from the Scriptures that there are a correlation and a conjunction of both the human and divine agencies in sanctification. To exclude or deemphasize one or the other is to miss an important aspect of the truth and to have an unbalanced, defective spirituality.

OTHER MEANS OF SANCTIFICATION

Not only do God and we have a part in the process of sanctification, but there are also several other means of grace revealed in the Scriptures.

1. The Word of God. We have already noticed that the Lord prayed that the Father would sanctify believers through the Word (John 17:17). The early church found it important to continue in the apostles' doctrine (Acts 2:42). Our Lord Himself serves as the finest example of the need for and proper use of the Word to meet temptation (Matt. 4:1-11). The heart of Paul's missionary journeys was the preaching of the Word of God (Acts 13:5, 44, 46; 17:2; 18:4; 20:32). The use of the Word is basic and crucial for sanctification.

This includes all aspects of the Word of God. Just as babies

desire the unadulterated milk of the mother's breast, so the believer should continually desire the pure, spiritual milk which is found in the Scriptures (I Peter 2:2). The phrase "as newborn babes" does not mean that the milk of the Word is only for recent converts. Rather it draws an analogy between what is the wish of every baby and what ought to be the longing of every believer. None of us ever outgrows his need for meditating on the basics of the Word. The problem is not that mature Christians avoid using the milk of the Word; rather, the usual problem is that immature Christians are content never to advance beyond the baby stage. Thus the "meat" truths of the Bible must also be a part of the believer's diet so that he may have a properly developed and soundly based spirituality.

There are two extremes to be avoided in one's use of the Bible in sanctification. The one might be labeled spiritual schizophrenia which is a "type of psychosis characterized by loss of contact with environment and by disintegration of personality." In other words, the spiritual schizophrenic is the person who never allows the Bible to make contact with the life situation in which he finds himself. His orthodoxy is without reproach but his orthopraxy leaves a lot to be desired. Or in the words of Scripture he is a hearer and not a doer of the Word. His knowledge of the Word is not integrated with his habits of living. We must never disunite doctrine from practice.

During my years of teaching I know that I have developed idiosyncrasies. I am certain that I am unaware of some of them, but one that I do know about is my invariable reaction to the chapel speaker who begins his message something like this: "Now today, young people, I'm going to be very practical in my message. I'll leave the doctrine to your teachers and the classroom— I just want to be practical." By this time I have already tuned the speaker out, for he has made a fundamental mistake in disjoining doctrine and practice. All doctrine is practical, and all practice must be based on sound doctrine. Doctrine that is not practical is not healthy doctrine, and practice that is not doctrinal is not rightly based.

Apparently it is men (in contrast to women) who particularly need this warning, for James declares that the one who looks into the Word and goes away without a change of life is like a

man (the Greek word used in James 1:23 is that which means the male) who looks in a mirror and promptly forgets what he sees. The illustration is all too pointed, for a man seeing something out of place when he looks in the mirror usually does not bother to remedy the situation. But nothing can pull a woman away from a mirror until she is completely satisfied that everything is in order. So it is, unfortunately, with the Bible. Men, being less sensitive, are less apt to be moved by the Word than women. Paul, too, speaks of the responsibility of men in this matter of knowing and practicing the Word. If women are supposed to ask their husbands biblical questions at home, this obviously presupposes that the husband will know the answers (I Cor. 14:35). Thus men in particular, but all believers too, need to know the Word and to put their knowledge into practice.

The other extreme to be avoided in one's use of the Bible is mysticism. Pseudospiritual people are often afflicted with this. Some of the symptoms are: "The Lord led me not to go to church"; "The Lord gave me such a wonderful thought this morning out of such-and-such a verse"—a thought which, upon examining the verse, is nowhere to be found; "I don't need anyone to teach me the Bible—the Holy Spirit is the only teacher I need." Of course, the Holy Spirit does teach us the meaning of the Word, and His ministry is indispensable (John 16:13; I Cor. 2:12). But the Bible does not say that His ministry of teaching will always be direct. Indeed, it is most often mediated through gifted teachers of the past and present whom God has given to the church. Sometimes this ministry may be direct as one persistently and intelligently searches out the meaning of a passage. But often it comes through the pastor's message or the teacher's lesson or a concordance or other books of men both living and dead.

To employ a purely mystical approach to the understanding of the Word can lead to several serious errors. For one thing, it can lead to ignorance of the Word since it may become an excuse for not studying the Word. One can wait until he is "given" something which may be utterly false simply because he does not know the true meaning of the passage upon which he is meditating. He can keep telling himself that the Lord has given him this special meaning and practically hypnotize himself into thinking this is the true meaning or some deeper meaning that

no one else has ever seen. The Scripture then becomes no longer a guide for our lives but an excuse for our actions.

Too, mysticism can lead to very strange if not false leading of the Lord. I have heard pseudospiritual people in places of leadership say that the Lord has led them not to attend the meetings of the church but rather to have their own home meetings in direct competition to the church where they still belong and which they serve when it suits their convenience. How tragic it is to see a student "led of the Lord" in some morning devotions to leave school (usually the morning is the day after he does poorly in an exam). What happened to the call of God on his life? What kind of leading was it when he was so sure that God had led him to that school? It is very easy to pass from a mystical meditation ungoverned by knowledge to saying "The Lord led me," and then to justify the action on the basis of ignorance of the Word. This is wishful thinking, not spiritual leading.

How, then, can I study the Word profitably so that the Lord may use it as a means of sanctifying my life? The answer is very simple: It must be read, understood and obeyed. The "secret" of doing the reading is persistence, and it is better to read something from the Word daily than to read a large portion weekly and nothing in between. My own opinion is that the new Christian should start with whatever book interests him, rather than trying to follow what someone else prescribes as the best plan. But the important thing is read, read, and keep reading.

As far as understanding the Word is concerned there are some things that will help. The first is a translation that is easier to understand than the King James Version. For some this will mean using one of the revised versions, while others may prefer one of the several good paraphrases in print today. But do not feel bound to the King James and its seventeenth century English.

Another very basic help to understanding the Bible—and one that is often overlooked—is an English dictionary. Words like ephah, ephod, spikenard and timbrel are all defined in the dictionary. Even more theological terms like Pentecost, church and mystery are given their theological meaning in the English dictionary. I am sure that many people do not understand the Bible simply because they do not know the meaning of the English words they are reading. (This is often painfully evident when

you hear someone read the Scriptures aloud as in a church service!)

When you understand the meaning of the words you are reading, then proceed on the assumption that they are to be understood plainly. Assume that God wanted to tell you something
through His Word and that He is not trying to confound or confuse you but He is speaking plainly to you. Do not look for "hidden meanings" or some "deeper" interpretation. Do not be concerned with what you do not yet understand but concern your-
self with what you plainly comprehend. As you persist, you will
discover that more and more of the Bible is becoming intelligible
to you.

If you want to understand the Bible more thoroughly, begin
to use some of the many excellent aids that are available today.
There are commentaries written for laymen that are good and,
in paperback, inexpensive. The use of a concordance will lead
you into truths that you did not know before. Simply take a
word (like *fear*, for instance) and trace its uses through the
Bible. A neighborhood Bible class or an evening school class
sponsored by a Bible institute will provide more formal training
and is a worthwhile investment of time and effort. Many Bible
institutes have correspondence courses which can be taken at
home at your own pace.

But, as we have noted before, knowledge without obedience is
fruitless. So let your reactions to that which you study be always
those that will draw you closer to God and never those which will
draw you away from Him. To the one who persists and obeys,
God will give increasing understanding of His truth and His will.
The Holy Spirit has been sent specifically to give us understanding of the things of Christ, and He who is the divine Author of
the Word will not fail in this work.

2. Prayer. A second means of sanctification is prayer. This, too,
was one of the characteristics of the early church (Acts 2:42; cf.
3:1; 4:24; 6:4; 9:40; 10:4, 31; 12:5; 13:3; 16:13, 16; 28:8), and it is
enjoined on believers. Our Lord said, "Men ought always to pray,
and not to faint" (Luke 18:1). The word *faint* means "to become disheartened or weary." The Apostle Paul commanded:
"Continue in prayer, and watch in the same with thanksgiving"
(Col. 4:2). He also said, "Pray without ceasing" (I Thess. 5:17).

Although these are familiar verses they do not say exactly the same thing. The word *always* used in Luke 18:1 is the usual word in the New Testament for always and means "in every situation and circumstance." The word *continue* in Colossians 4:2 is a compound verb built on a root which means "strength" and comes to mean "give strength" to your praying. Or we might translate it "be devoted to prayer" or even "give your energy to prayer." The idea is simply that we are to be energetic in prayer. The concept of praying without ceasing (I Thess. 5:17) is analogous to having a hacking cough. Indeed the word is used in that way outside the New Testament. Now when you have a hacking cough you do not actually cough all the time although you feel the cough always present in your throat. The chronic condition is there continually, but it only erupts in coughing at certain times. This is what is meant by praying without ceasing. The attitude of prayerfulness should be with us all the time, and that attitude will erupt many times during the course of a day. Prayer is a vital means of sanctification.

But the practical problem most have in praying is knowing how to pray in the will of God so that we may expect answers. Prayer promises always contain a condition—"according to his will" (I John 5:14), "believing" (Matt. 21:22), "if ye abide in me, and my words abide in you" (John 15:7). Thus to picture prayer as God giving the believer a blank check is to present only part of the total picture. Even a blank check has to be filled in properly in order to be cashed. And to fill in a check one must know certain things such as how to write, what date it is, and what is the proper amount to fill in. No bank would cash a blank check even if it had been signed. It must be correctly filled in. Then it can be cashed even though the handwriting of the signature is different from that on the rest of the check. Likewise, God does not answer prayers that are presented in blank even though He has signed the check. There are conditions which we must meet in our praying.

An illustration of an uncommon situation may help understand what it means to pray in the name of Christ. When I was preparing to go abroad to study I had to see to it that my affairs would be cared for while I was out of the country. It was necessary to see to it that I could get money easily and to look after a little

property that I owned. To facilitate these matters I signed a document, called a power of attorney. It was a lengthy and detailed document, and it gave my father as my attorney the right to do anything in my name. Of course, a power of attorney may be executed to cover only a specific matter. But mine was as all-inclusive as I could make it so that whatever came up in my absence could be handled by my father-attorney. I confess that when I first read the document I was startled to see how much power I was placing in the hands of someone else, even though that someone was my own father. He could have borrowed money in my name, and I would have been responsible. He could have sold or bought property in my name, and I would have been responsible. He could have taken an expensive vacation and signed the checks in my name, and I would have been responsible. I had given him blanket power, but I was not a bit concerned. For I knew that my father would never have done anything that I would not have approved of. It was a blank check, but I trusted him to fill it in as I would have.

Prayer promises are like a power of attorney, but this power will never be misused by a child of God who is in fellowship with his heavenly Father. If we try to misuse it, God, who is ultimately in control of all things, will deny our petition and try to bring us to the place where we will know how to use it properly. When His words abide in us we will ask only what He would want—we will exercise His power only as He would. When you kneel to use the power of attorney God has given you, you will ask, "What does God want in this situation?" or "What will be best for His interests?" This is asking according to His will. This is asking in faith which means certain trust based on knowledge of His will. Faith is not generated by a kind of repetitious self-hypnosis; rather, it is strengthened through a knowledge of the one in whom it is placed, and that kind of knowledge comes through studying God's Word and through experiences with Him as we go through life.

3. Fellowship and worship. In addition to emphasizing doctrine and prayer, the early church also continued steadfast in fellowship and breaking of bread. Both of these, of course, have to do with the corporate worship of the church which is another means of sanctification. "Many coals make a good fire," said

Samuel Rutherford, and the Bible affirms the need of group fellowship. The writer to the Hebrews reminded his readers: "And let us consider one another to provoke unto love and to good works: not forsaking the assembling of ourselves together, as the manner of some is; but exhorting one another: and so much the more, as ye see the day approaching" (10:24-25). Group worship should include exhortation (Heb. 10:25), edification (I Cor. 14:26), observance of the Lord's Supper (Acts 20:7; I Cor. 11:17 ff.), reading of the Word of God (Col. 4:16), witness to the unsaved (I Cor. 14:24), preaching by special speakers (Acts 20:7), disciplining (I Cor. 5:4-5), and general exercise of spiritual gifts (I Cor. 12–14). All of these things are necessary to advance the spiritual life, and they are to be practiced by the local church.

Sometimes you will run across an unbalanced view of the victorious life which disparages the local church and its activities. Such a viewpoint goes something like this: Since the early church met in homes we ought to also. Too, they often add, the churches do not appreciate our emphasis on the victorious life, so we will be obliged to specialize on that teaching in our home meetings. Such specialization usually centers on a particular man or group or the writings of either.

The error of such teaching is twofold. First of all, the early church met in homes simply because they could not erect buildings in which to assemble. The place of meeting is not a distinguishing characteristic of a local church. The character of the people as professed believers, the presence of organization in the persons of elders and deacons, the purpose of the group to carry out the Great Commission, are the things which distinguish a local church from just a group of believers who get together somewhere. In the second place, such unorganized groups of people meeting together to promote their view of the victorious life usually are in error because they do not study and proclaim the whole counsel of God (Acts 20:27). Often, too, they do not even try to evangelize; rather they proselytize from other Christian groups. Therefore, since they usually do not carry out the God-ordained purposes of a local church, they do not qualify as such even though they meet in a house as they had to do in apostolic times. God places a great deal of emphasis on the local church in the New Testament; therefore, we should hold

suspect any teaching that in any way diminishes that emphasis.

A vital part of the worship of the church is the observance of the ordinances. In and of themselves baptism and the Lord's Supper do not impart grace, but they may be used of the Spirit as instruments through which blessing and help may come to believers. Baptism should remind those who are baptized and those who watch of their union with Christ with its newness of life (Rom. 6:1-10). In the Lord's Supper we remember the Lord, both in the perfection of His life and in the efficacy of His death. Proper preparation for the supper includes self-examination and confession of known sin (I Cor. 11:27-32), and it goes without saying that if this is practiced it is a very important contribution to practical sanctification. It is clear that these ordinances can be means for our sanctification; the tragedy is that so often today they are performed as a matter of routine, with the average church member scarcely involved with their significance.

4. Other means of sanctification. Undoubtedly a list of means of sanctification could grow very lengthy, for actually every activity and circumstance of life may be used to draw us closer to God. Acknowledging the blessings of common grace will promote a thankful spirit. Natural talents may be used for the Lord's glory, bringing blessing to both user and those who benefit. The union of husband and wife which carries the analogy of the relationship between Christ and His church ought to be a constant reminder to live as would please Him. The relationship between parents and children, employers and employees, governors and governed, could be means of purifying the life. Indeed, every circumstance can be a vehicle of good for the children of God (Rom. 8:28). "His grace has infinite horizons, and the agencies through which it is conveyed are as varied and multiform as life itself."[2]

There can be no question about the limitless and manifold provision of God's grace; He does His part. But, as we have seen, man must also do his part. Although God is able to use relationships and circumstances to our good, we can frustrate the grace of God in these matters. Thus it is imperative that we be conscious of the fact that God is working through varied experiences

2. Frank E. Gaebelein, "Other Means of Grace," *Basic Christian Doctrines,* p. 267.

of life and that we seek to learn the lessons He has for us. A very practical suggestion in this regard is this: Try praying daily that every reaction to each event of that day will be such as will draw you closer to the Lord and never away from Him. Ask Him to put a brake on those feelings and attitudes which would hinder His ministering grace through all the situations which you face each day. Means of grace for our sanctification are all about us; let us use them to the fullest for His glory.

7

DEDICATION

THERE IS PERHAPS no more important matter in relation to the spiritual life than dedication. And yet this very basic concept is often confused especially when it is made a part of "formulas" for victorious living. Some present dedication as the entire answer to all the problems of the Christian life; others give it little place; and most do not understand the place of rededication in the whole matter. To be confused at this point is to do damage to the entire biblical teaching on Christian living.

THE BASIS OF DEDICATION

Throughout Scripture the call to dedication is always based on blessings already granted. In other words, God appeals to His children to dedicate their lives on the basis of the fact that He has richly blessed them. In both Testaments the blessings are related to the position of His people, either in the commonwealth of Israel or in the church, the body of Christ. Although there are many "mercies of God" which should motivate the believer to dedication, probably the chief one in the background of dedication is redemption. The "mercies of God" of Romans 12:1, which are Paul's basis for appeal for the presentation of one's body as a living sacrifice, certainly include the two previous mentions of redemption. In Romans 3:24 the apostle has reminded his readers that their position in Christ as justified by a righteous God is "through the redemption that is in Christ Jesus." In 8:23 he looks ahead to the redemption of the Christian's body. The same appeal is made in I Corinthians 6:19-20: "What? Know ye not that your body is the temple of the Holy Ghost which is in you, which ye have of God, and ye are not your own? For ye are bought with a price: therefore glorify God in your body." The word translated

as *bought* is the Greek word for *redeem;* thus redemption is made the basis again for the exhortation to glorify God in our bodies.

Since redemption is so basic to dedication, it would not be amiss to look into some of the things involved in this concept. The New Testament teaching concerning redemption is based on three words which are used to convey the concept. The first is a simple word which means to buy or purchase or pay a price for something. It is used, for instance, with this ordinary, everyday meaning in the parable of the treasure hid in a field which motivated the man to buy (redeem) the field (Matt. 13:44). In relation to our salvation, the word means to pay the price which our sin demands so that we can be redeemed (Rev. 5:9; II Peter 2:1). And it is only by the blood of Christ that the price can be paid.

The second word for redemption is the same first basic word prefixed with a preposition. This has the force of intensifying the meaning in a way that can easily be translated into English, for the prepositional prefix is the little word that means "out of." Since the root of the word *redemption* is the word for the marketplace (thus to pay the price in the market), this second word means to purchase out of the market. In other words, the idea in this second word is that the death of Christ not only paid the price for our salvation but also removed us from the marketplace of sin in order to give assurance to us that we will never be returned to the bondage and penalties of sin. Christ's coming was in order "to redeem them that were under the law, that we might receive the adoption of sons" (Gal. 4:5). The use of this compound word in this verse assures us that we can never lose that adoption as sons and be returned to bondage.

The third word for redemption is an entirely different Greek word, and it signifies that the purchased person is also released and set free in the fullest sense. Again it is Paul who says that the death of Christ was in order that "he might redeem us from all iniquity, and purify unto himself a peculiar people, zealous of good works" (Titus 2:14). Thus, redemption in its fullest connotation means that because of the shedding of the blood of Christ believers have been purchased, removed and liberated.

Since redemption includes this idea of freedom, this means that the child of God is not automatically a servant of the new

Master who bought him. If that were so, then the sinner's bondage would only have been transferred from one master (sin) to another (Christ). The truth is that Christ has purchased us in order that we might be free, and He does not take unwilling servants or slaves into captivity. That accounts for the exhortations, rather than commands, which we read in the New Testament to offer ourselves willingly to the Lord in dedication of life. Or to put it another way, those who have been set free from the slavery of sin are asked to enter voluntarily into a new servitude, and the request is made on the basis of the very act that set them free. The awesome purchase price of the very life of the Son of God should be more than ample motivation to make every child of God eagerly want to yield back to the Lord the very freedom which His death bought.

All of this is beautifully illustrated in one of the regulations of the Mosaic law. The Hebrew slave who was to be set free by his Hebrew master the seventh year might choose to stay in the service of that master for the remainder of his life. Of course this choice was entirely voluntary on the part of the slave, but if the relationship of life servitude was entered into, then the agreement was sealed by the master piercing the ear of the slave with an awl. "And it shall be, if he say unto thee, I will not go away from thee; because he loveth thee and thine house, because he is well with thee; then thou shalt take an aul, and thrust it through his ear unto the door, and he shall be thy servant for ever. And also unto thy maidservant thou shalt do likewise" (Deut. 15:16-17). Notice the two reasons why a man might make a choice like this: because he loved the master and because the master had been good to him. The mercies of God, the basis for our dedication, are far greater than those of any human master, and blessings of a life dedicated in service to God are far more certain in their richness. Why so many hesitate to dedicate themselves to Him is difficult to understand.

THE AREA OF DEDICATION

What is it that the Christian is to dedicate? The answer is himself. "Yield yourselves unto God" (Rom. 6:13), "present your bodies" (Rom. 12:1), "glorify God in your body" (I Cor. 6:20), "submit yourselves . . . to God" (James 4:7)—this is the uniform

appeal of Scripture, and it concerns our bodies. If this is so, then it follows that dedication concerns the years of one's life, since that is the only period in which the body functions. Dedication concerns the present life, not the life hereafter.

Very often these days dedication is mixed up with salvation. We must not digress on this point too long except to say that salvation concerns my personal relationship to Jesus Christ as my Substitute for sin which unless paid for would bring me into eternal condemnation. Dedication concerns the subjection of my life to Jesus Christ as long as I live. Salvation involves the sin question; dedication, subjection. But too often victorious life speakers make dedication a condition for salvation, and this is nothing less than adding works to the grace of God. We shall look into this more fully in a later chapter.

If dedication concerns the years of one's life, it is directed primarily to the question of the control of that life. Simply stated, dedication concerns whether I will direct my life or whether Christ will. Dedication only secondarily concerns the issues or details of life, and yet these are frequently made the substance of dedication. What I am saying is this: Dedication does not pose the question of whether, for instance, one will go to the mission field; nor does it ask whether one will turn over his business to the Lord. It faces the Christian with the question of who will be the master of the years of his life. Once that is decided then the question of the mission field or business as well as every other detail of life has automatically been involved in that basic decision.

Now it is true that often the Holy Spirit will face a Christian with the basic question of control through one of the secondary questions of detail. Frequently it is some business decision or lifework decision which brings to the forefront the issue of mastery of the entire life. But dedication should never be presented as a matter of yielding to some *thing* or in some *area;* it should always be directed toward *someone,* the Lord Himself.

To dedicate in some area or in relation to some thing will, of course, mean that only that area or thing in life has been yielded to the Lord's control. Then in the course of time another problem or decision will face the person, and he will have to decide whether or not to yield to the Lord's will in that respect. Then

another choice will arise. Then a crossroads will appear, and so on and on through life. Each time the believer will be faced with deciding his basic relationship to the will of God. It will be like weeding a garden. This year you pull up one weed; another year, another. In the meantime more weeds grow, and there is never any basic settledness toward the will of God. But if one dedicates his life with all of its problems, decisions, situations and circumstances—both known and unknown—as decisions arise they can always be faced in light of the fact that there has been a basic, total and lifelong commitment to the will of God.

Thus the area of dedication is one's whole life. This will involve the details of life, but it involves them not as means to dedication but as results of dedication.

THE COMPONENTS OF DEDICATION

The dedicated life (the initial act of dedication plus continuous commitment to it) involves at least three component features. They are clearly delineated in Romans 12:1-2 which is undoubtedly the central and favorite (though not always correctly interpreted) passage on the subject.

1. The dedicated life must be initiated by the believer by presenting himself as a living sacrifice. Paul addresses his readers as brethren; yet he feels it necessary to urge them to make that presentation or dedication. While the aorist tense itself does not indicate whether the action referred to is past, present, or future, obviously here it does not indicate past action. Otherwise Paul would not need to urge them to make this since they would already have done it. Rather he is urging them to make a presentation which they had not previously made. Furthermore, the presentation of body is reasonable or rational or logical in view of the greatness of the mercies of God in salvation. Too, it is a sacrificial thing since we are asked to live for Christ in the daily routine as well as in the more unusual occurrences of life. We are to be living sacrifices, not dead ones. And, of course, this presentation is to be a complete one. It involves all of our bodies, or, as Paul puts it in 6:13, "present yourselves." This means clearly a total presentation, not a partial one, and it includes all that we know about ourselves at the time of presentation and all the unknown future. It includes the good that we possess as well as the bad. We do

not give over to the Lord just those aspects of our lives which we cannot control or which we wish to rid ourselves of, but we give Him everything including the good traits and talents. And all is for Him to use or not to use as He sees fit. This is the logical, sacrificial, total and decisive presentation of dedication.

2. The dedicated life also involves a separation or a nonconformity to the evil age in which we live (Gal. 1:4). Perhaps we can understand what nonconformity is by looking at the opposite. The character of conformity is really hypocrisy, for the meaning of the word used here is that the outward appearance looks similar to that of the world even though the transformation of the new birth has taken place within the heart. Conformity, then, is two-facedness, and it is something similar to Satan's character, because he, although inwardly a liar from the beginning, is able to transform himself into a veritable angel of light (II Cor. 11:14; this is the same root word). It is tragic but true that too many believers, although children of light, are covered with the veneer of this present age.

The meaning of nonconformity involves the idea of being unfashionable. The only other occurrence of the Greek word used in Romans 12:2a gives us the hint for using this word *unfashionable* in defining the concept. Peter uses it in I Peter 1:14 and it is translated "not fashioning yourselves." This is a very vivid expression and throws the light of God's Word on so many of our ambitions, activities, goals, standards and programs which are too often geared to the methods of the day rather than to the glory of God. Separation from the world, or nonconformity, is being unfashionable, and this is a necessary characteristic of the dedicated life.

3. The third feature of the dedicated life is transformation. Both separation and transformation are required. The one is negative and the other is positive. The one is more outward; the other, inward. The positive transformation is done by the Holy Spirit (II Cor. 3:18) but the center of it is the mind. This is rather unexpected, for we would more naturally think of the need for cleansed hearts or lives, rather than minds. And yet in this passage it is the mind that is the center of the transforming activity of the Spirit in the life of the believer. Too often we think of total depravity as affecting man from his neck down, and we

unconsciously exempt the head from the effects of sin. Consequently, we conclude that what we think or the attitudes we have are free from the effects of the fall. This is not so, and the fact that the transformation of life centers in the mind demonstrates this. We need to think God's standards in order to have our lives transformed into His likeness. He who is light, holiness and truth is our standard, not the world with all of its counterfeits. In summarizing the need for separation and transformation the church father, Tertullian, put it this way: "But our Lord Christ has surnamed Himself Truth, not custom."

THE FREQUENCY OF DEDICATION

Does the act of dedication have to be repeated? Enough has already been said to indicate that this author believes not. The use of the aorist tense in these dedication verses alone would argue for such a conclusion. Only the preaching of many victorious life speakers and the apparent need of many Christians seem to argue for rededication. What is the truth about this matter?

The scriptural picture is an initial act of dedication which includes all of oneself for all of one's life. This should never be taken back; therefore, when a dedicated person comes to a crossroads in life or faces a decision, he is not faced with deciding again whether or not he will do the will of God. This has already and forever been decided in that crisis dedication. He only must find what the will of God is in this situation; then he will gladly do it. This is the biblical picture of a dedicated life. But, of course, when Christians come to such crossroads and decisions they sometimes choose not to do what they know to be the will of God. In such instances, sin enters and their dedication has been violated. They miss the will of God and substitute their own will in the particular situation. They may be out of the will of God in a major area or in a minor area of life, but in either case they have gone back on their dedication vow.

What is needed in such cases to remedy the situation? Is it a rededication? In a sense one might call it that, but it is a use of the basic word *dedication* with a different connotation. The rededication (if one calls it that) is not a doing again of the same thing that was done at the time of dedication; therefore, the re-

dedication connotes something different from dedication. In such a usage, rededication means getting back on the track on which you started at the time of dedication. It would probably be better to call the remedy restoration, and this comes through confession of sin. Choosing to do your own will even though dedicated is a very real possibility since God does not remove from us the freedom of choice when we dedicate ourselves to Him. When we wish to recognize and admit that we have thus sinned, the remedy is not rededication but confession of the sin and restoration to the place of fellowship. Then we can go on living a dedicated life. It is not necessary to start over; and even though sin leaves its mark, it does not always mean that everything is lost. Confession and restoration may, therefore, be frequent in the dedicated Christian's life. Indeed, they will occur in every Christian's life as long as we live in these bodies. But a rededication (meaning doing again the same thing that was done in dedication) is really not an accurate way to express the remedy.

But if rededication is not really a wrong concept (if it means restoration), why quibble over the use of the word? This is why. In practice a rededication emphasis gives one the picture of needing to pluck out this sin, get rid of that wrong, change that fault, so that if you rededicate often enough you will eventually become dedicated. Rededication becomes a means of dedication, not a route to restoration. This is why the emphasis often becomes confusing if not damaging to normal Christian growth. Every speaker is tempted to prefer to see a lot of decisions about particular problems in lives than to have one genuine, complete, crisis dedication, and this is why rededication is so often preached. But it is far better to be clear concerning the completeness of dedication, to be pointed in asking people on which side of the dedication line they stand, and to clarify the difference between genuine dedication and a violation of dedication which requires confession and restoration to remedy.

So let me take my own advice and be clear and pointed. Each believer stands on one side or the other of dedication. Either we have made this lifelong commitment or we have not. Either we have faced the issue of who is to be the master of our lives or we have been plucking up one sin at a time. If there has never been a dedication of life this is the next step the reader should

take. If there has been, then it is always profitable to examine the present state of that dedicated life. If in any area one's dedication has for any reason been violated, then the remedy is confession to God and restoration by God. This, too, can be done at any time—even while reading these words.

The Results of Dedication

There are many detailed results of dedication, but we want here to concentrate on those results in two major areas of life. Dedication, first of all, relates to the will of God. Romans 12:2 says that the result of presentation, separation and transformation is "that ye may prove what is that good, and acceptable, and perfect, will of God." This means that dedication brings the knowledge, the doing and the enjoying of God's will for that life. A life lived in the light of the will of God is not a sinless life, but it is a life directed in the right path; it is a life that grows and matures day by day.

But dedication is also related to the filling of the Spirit. To be filled with the Spirit is to be controlled by the Spirit. To dedicate one's life to God is to yield control to Him. Thus dedication allows the Holy Spirit to fill the life of the believer. An undedicated life reserves control for self and thus prevents the Spirit's filling that person. Of course, if dedication is violated, the filling ministry of the Spirit is hindered; but without initial dedication there can be no real experience of this vital ministry of the Spirit. Thus dedication is a prerequisite for being filled with the Spirit; this is not all that is involved, but the rest of the story must await another chapter.

These are some aspects of dedication and the dedicated life. This is the starting place for the victorious life. Without it there is no victory; with it the basis for victory is laid.

8

MONEY AND THE LOVE OF GOD

ONE OF THE MOST IMPORTANT evidences of true spirituality is seldom discussed in books or sermons on the subject. We are prone to paint the image of spirituality in colors of deep Bible knowledge, lengthy times of prayer, or prominence in the Lord's work, which is not only deceiving but must be very discouraging to the average believer who can never envision these features as being a part of his life. He concludes, therefore, that these major manifestations of spirituality will never be seen in his life.

To be sure, a vital spiritual life is related to fellowship with the Lord in His Word and prayer and to service for the Lord in His work. But our love for God may be proved by something that is a major part of everyone's life, and that is our use of money. How we use our money demonstrates the reality of our love for God. In some ways it proves our love more conclusively than depth or knowledge, length of prayers or prominence of service. These things can be feigned, but the use of our possessions shows us up for what we actually are.

GIVING

The Apostle John links money and the love of God: "But whoso hath this world's good, and seeth his brother have need, and shutteth up his . . . [heart] from him, how dwelleth the love of God in him?" (I John 3:17). This verse is preceded by one which says we ought to lay down our lives for the brethren in order to give the ultimate proof of love. But, of course, most Christians will never have the opportunity to do this even if they would seize the opportunity if it came. How, then, can the believer in ordinary circumstances show that he loves his brother and thus God? The answer is simple: By giving money and goods to his

brother. If he fails to do this, then he shows not only that he does not love his brother but also that he does not love God. There is scarcely anyone who cannot give; therefore, all can show by this means the measure of their love for God. Giving of money and things is a manifestation and responsibility of a truly spiritual life.

How, then, do we properly discharge this responsibility?

Without apology the New Testament places a great deal of emphasis on the subject of giving. There are commands, practical suggestions, warnings, examples and exhortations concerning this important ministry. Everywhere in the Bible miserliness, greed and avarice are denounced; and generosity, hospitality and charity are extolled. Money is not a carnal or worldly subject to be avoided or spoken of only after "more important" matters have been considered. The same word that is used for our fellowship with the Lord is also used in relation to the fellowship of collecting money (II Cor. 8:4). This clearly underlines the spiritual character of giving. Furthermore, giving is a spiritual gift (Rom. 12:8) which is available to all believers to have and to use. And it is a gift which all Christians can exercise regardless of the individual's financial status.

There is always a tendency when we read the Bible passages that speak of money or rich people to apply them to someone else. We invariably look at the person in the next higher income bracket and transfer the teaching of such passages to him. We too easily forget that there is someone in the next lower income range who is looking at us and applying the teaching to us! Each of us is a rich person to someone else; therefore, these teachings apply to all of us.

What should be one's guide in grace giving? Undoubtedly the New Testament passage which sets forth most concisely the basic principles of giving is I Corinthians 16:2: "Upon the first day of the week let every one of you lay by him in store, as God hath prospered him, that there be no gatherings when I come." In this single verse are laid down four principles of giving.

1. Giving is incumbent on each person—*let every one of you.* Grace does not make giving optional; it is the privilege and responsibility of every Christian, and it is the concrete manifestation of his love for God. Giving is a personal matter in which every

believer sustains a direct and individual responsibility to the Lord as if he were the only Christian in the world. What you give is your personal business just as long as you are giving and doing it in conference with Him before whom all things are naked and open.

2. Giving is to be proportionate—"as God hath prospered him." No hard and fast rule concerning the amount is to be found among New Testament principles of giving. This is in sharp contrast to the regulations of the Old Testament which required that a tenth of all be given to the Levites (Lev. 27:30-33), who in turn tithed what they received and gave it to the priests. In addition, the Jews understood that a second tithe (a tenth of the remaining nine-tenths) was to be set apart and consumed in a sacred meal in Jerusalem (Deut. 12:5-6, 11, 18; those living too far from Jerusalem could bring money). Further, every third year another tithe was taken for the Levites, strangers, fatherless and widows (Deut. 14:28-29). Thus the proportion was clearly specified and every Israelite was obligated to bring to the Lord approximately 22 percent of his yearly income. In contrast, the New Testament merely says "as God hath prospered him." This may mean 8, 12, 20, 50 percent—any percent, depending on the individual case. It may also mean a variation in proportion from year to year, for there is no reason to believe that the proportion suitable for one year will be satisfactory for the next. When prosperity comes, as it has for many Christians, it should be used to give more, not necessarily to buy more. Each time the Christian gives he is to reflect on God's blessing in his life and determine what proportion in return he will give to God. A variation in the proportion means just this—not an increase or decrease merely in the amount given, but a change in the proportion of one's income which is given to the Lord (which of course will also change the amount).

3. Giving is to be in private deposit—"lay by him in store." Contrary to the usual belief, the Christian is not told to turn his gift into the church treasury each Sunday. The Greek word *in store* means to gather and lay up, to heap up, to treasure; and the reflexive pronoun *to himself* indicates that the gift is to be kept in private, not public, deposit. The picture in this verse is clearly of a private gift fund into which the believer places his propor-

tionately determined gifts and out of which he distributes to specific causes. This does not mean that either the giving into such a fund or the paying out from such a fund is spasmodic. Neither does it mean that regular giving or even pledging is contrary to the New Testament principles of giving (cf. II Cor. 8:10-11 where a pledge was made and where Paul exhorted them to fulfill their pledge). But it does mean that there should be, however small, an ever-ready supply of money available to give out as the Spirit directs, both regularly and occasionally.

4. Giving should be periodic—"on the first day of the week." It has already been pointed out that giving is not an erratic business. The laying by in private store should be done on Sunday. The Lord's Day is God's appointed day for keeping accounts, determining proportions, and laying by in store. The Scriptures do not say much about what the Christian should or should not do on Sunday except that he should assemble with other believers in worship (Heb. 10:25) and do his giving (I Cor. 16:2). Although one need not become ritualistic about this matter of caring for our giving to the Lord on Sunday, neither should it be treated lightly. Here is a God-given command which we would do well to heed. I have made a practice of doing this, and strange as it may seem, doing it on the Lord's Day seems to bring an added blessing. Often, too, the Lord's Day provides a better time away from the distractions of the duties of the week to think more clearly and carefully about this important matter. One of my students tried this one year and testified to the blessing it brought to his family; for, gathered together as a family group on Sunday afternoon thinking and praying together about their giving to the Lord, their spiritual ties were strengthened. If God has suggested it, it is certainly worth trying.

But, someone will say, why go to all this trouble? Why not just take a tithe out of every paycheck and place it in the collection plate the following Sunday? The word *tithe* is found in the New Testament only eight times (Matt. 23:23; Luke 11:42; 18:12; Heb. 7:5-6, 8-9). In the references in the Gospels it is used in connection with that which the Pharisees were doing in fulfilling their obligation to the Mosaic law. In the references in Hebrews tithing is used to prove the inferiority of the Levitical priesthood to the Melchizedek priesthood. Since Levi paid tithes in Abra-

ham when Abraham met Melchizedek, he demonstrates the recognized superiority of Melchizedek and of his priesthood. The passage does not go on and say (as is often implied) that we Christians, therefore, should pay tithes to Christ our High Priest.

It is apparent that the tithe was part of the Mosaic law (Lev. 27:30-33) and an important factor in the economy of Israel. The law was never given to Gentiles and is expressly done away for the Christian (Rom. 2:14; II Cor. 3:7-13; Heb. 7:11-12). Neither are the words of Malachi 3 for the Christian, for what believer claims to be a son of Jacob to whom the passage is addressed (v. 6)? Furthermore, material blessing is never promised today as an automatic reward for faithfulness in any area of Christian living, including giving. Spiritual blessing (Eph. 1:3) and the meeting of material needs (Phil. 4:19) are what God promises. Being prospered materially is no necessary sign of deep godliness of faithful tithing; and contrariwise, poverty is no indication of being out of God's will (cf. Paul's own case in Phil. 4:12).

But, it may be asked, since tithing was practiced before the law, does not that fact make irrelevant all that has been said above and leave tithing as the proper principle to follow in giving? Since Abraham and Jacob both tithed, and since their acts antedated the law, does that not relieve tithing of its legal aspects and make it a valid principle to follow today? The answer would be yes if there were no other guides for giving in the New Testament. If the New Testament were silent on the matter, then of course we would seek for guidance anywhere we could find it in the Bible; but since the New Testament gives us clear principles to govern our giving, there is no need to go back to two isolated examples in the Old Testament for guidance. The fact that something was done before the law which was later incorporated into the law does not necessarily make that thing a good example for today, especially if the New Testament gives further guidance on the matter. Not even the most ardent tither would say that the Sabbath should be observed today because it was observed before the law (Exodus 16:23-36), yet this is the very reasoning used in promoting tithing today. The New Testament teaches us about a new day of worship, and it also gives us new directions for giving. To tithe today following the examples of those who did it before the law would mean that only 10 percent of one's in-

come would go to the Lord and only on certain occasions; to tithe on the basis of the teaching of the law would mean that 22 percent would be given to the Lord as payment of what was owed Him; but to give on the basis of the principles of the New Testament might mean any percent, and given in recognition that 100 percent belongs to Him. The Lord's work will never lack support if we preach and practice New Testament principles of giving.

Proportionate giving is not starting with a tithe and then doing what more we can when we can. Proportionate giving is giving as God hath prospered. If someone felt after prayer that the right proportion for him should be 10 percent, I would suggest that he give 9 or 11 percent just to keep out of the 10 percent rut. A person who is giving 9 or 11 percent will find himself much more sensitive to the Lord's changing his proportion than if he were giving 10 percent.

Every believer owes 100 percent of what he is and what he has to God. The question, then, is not only how much I give, but also how much I spend on myself. Proportionate giving alone can furnish the right answer to this matter and for every stage of life. We give because He gave, not because He commanded; we give because we want to, not because we have to; we give because we love Him, and we show that love most concretely in this way. If in turn God blesses us materially, we praise Him; if not, we still praise Him. This is grace giving, and this is the proof of our love for God.

Years ago Lewis Sperry Chafer wrote some choice words on the subject "Spirit-directed Giving." He defined this as "depending only on the Spirit of God to direct the gifts in the case of every person, and then being willing to abide by the results of this confidence and trust." Although not denying the need to be well informed about needs, he expressed the fear that "too many of our churches have been trained to respond only to the insistent human appeal, and this, like some medicine, requires an ever-increasing dose to produce the desired effect." Practicing this principle of information without solicitation, D. M. Stearns used to read to his congregation messages from Christian workers and then instruct his people to withhold their gifts unless not to give would burden their souls. "How jealously the giver should guard against any and all forms of human pressure which might mislead

him away from the discharge of his God-given responsibility, which responsibility is to find and to do the precise will of God! . . . Is your giving in obedience to the still, small voice of the Spirit of God? Are you, too, a part of the great, divine faith system?" This is grace giving, because it is Spirit-directed giving, and it is one of the most blessed experiences a believer may have.

BUYING

But giving is only half the story of money and our love for God. If everything comes from the Lord and belongs to Him, and if we have dedicated ourselves to Him, then not only is what we give to Him important but also what we spend on ourselves as indicative of our love. It is fallacious reasoning to think that when we have given a portion of our income to the Lord the rest belongs to us. It is all His; we merely use part of it for ourselves.

Although the average family's income is up considerably from what it was a few years ago, the universal complaint is "I do not have enough money." Everyone seems to want more, which, of course, is not wrong in itself. One wonders, however, for what purpose people want more money. It seems that very few have this goal in order to be able to increase their giving to the Lord's work. When all things are considered the purpose in too many cases seems to be to have more things. Today, the abundant economic life has become the necessary life.

But, someone may be thinking, what is wrong with having more material goods? What is so evil about the luxuries of the past generation becoming the necessities of this present generation? Is that not progress? And does not God want us to enjoy all things? After all, the Bible does not condemn things—just the love of things.

Unquestionably, the Christian's use of money is the object of pulls and pressures from every side, whether it be from the advertising industry, from our own desires, or from the world around us. Every child of God needs help in discovering what is right and what is wrong in the use of money, particularly in an age of prosperity and full employment. If times were hard and money were tight, many of the problems would automatically disappear. It is an often overlooked truism that it is easier to live by faith when you do *not* have any money than when you do. After all,

when you have nothing, you have little choice about how to live.
You are much more inclined, if not actually forced, to live in
total dependence on the Lord. But when you have money in the
bank, you have a choice. You can spend it by faith or you can
spend it directed by self. Thus in a situation of plenty, it becomes most important to use properly the wealth that God gives
us.

What does the Bible say about the use of money? Are luxuries
worldly? May I have a new car, even a big car, in the will of
God, for instance? Of course, the Bible does not say whether so
many particular things are right or wrong to buy and have. But
the Scriptures do give some plain principles that should govern
the use of all money, for God is not simply concerned with the
percent we give to Him but with 100 percent of what we possess.

The passage of Scripture which gives us these principles is
seldom thought of when money is mentioned; it is I Timothy 6.
An interesting feature of I Timothy is the connection between
false teachers and money. And yet it is not a surprising connection, for false teachers usually are selfish in their desire for money,
and false doctrine will affect the proper use of money as quickly
as any aspect of living. An unscriptural attitude toward money
is a great spiritual peril.

In contrast to the teaching of the false teachers, Paul's overall
governing principle in regard to wealth is this: "Godliness with
contentment is great gain" (I Tim. 6:6). Great gain does not
necessarily come from two cars in the garage, but it comes from
godliness and contentment. This word *gain* means "basic necessities." Godliness with contentment is the basic necessity of the
Christian's life. No matter what else a man has, unless he has
this, he has only a superstructure without a foundation.

What is godliness? It includes at least what Paul describes in
verse 11 as righteousness, faith, love, patience and meekness.
Contentment includes those inner resources placed in the believer's life by grace, which will make him contented within the
varying moods and circumstances of life. It is the contentment of
knowing "how to be abased, and . . . how to abound" (Phil. 4:12).
This does not mean that a man should not try to improve his lot
in life, but it does mean that contentment involves learning to
love the will of God regardless of the circumstances into which it

may bring a person. In want content, and in plenty content—remembering that it is sometimes more difficult to be content in plenty than in want. This is the first great principle to guide the believer through the maze of the abundant life.

In terms of everyday living, this principle means, among other things, that the acquisition of the latest gadgets is not the most important matter in life. The believer who is not thus surrounded with the latest of everything should not be frustrated even if neighbors and other Christians look on the outward appearance, for God still looks on the heart. In His children's hearts the Lord wants first of all to find godliness with contentment. Buying too much may be a demonstration of our love for things and a proof of our lack of love for God.

Lest anyone think that this principle justifies idling in pious meditation all day without giving attention to financial responsibilities, Paul makes it abundantly clear that the Christian is obliged to support his minister (I Tim. 5:17-18) and his family (5:8). Failing to do this is to class oneself worse than an infidel.

Another great principle in this chapter is this: Do not love money or what it can buy. "For the love of money is the root of all evil" (6:10). On the one hand it means that the Christian must not covet money or the things it can buy. On the other hand, the injunction does not say that the Christian should not enjoy the things that God gives him if they are placed in proper perspective and bought in the will of God. Important, too, is the fact that this verse does not say that money itself is evil but only that one's attitude toward it may be evil. Indeed, Paul says in this very chapter that God has given us all things to enjoy (v. 17). Some fraudulently pious people are proud or falsely humble over what they do not have! No false humility or even sense of shame is warranted if *God* gives you something. And if it is something new in the will of God, be thankful, enjoy it, and do not be ashamed of having something nice and new. On the other hand, if last year's model has to do when other Christians have the latest, let godliness with contentment, not the love of things, rule the heart. It is important, too, to remember that getting something at a discount does not necessarily make it right. Things can be wrong at any price.

Of course, many "things" are without moral character in them-

selves. It is the believer's attitude toward things and not the things themselves that constitutes good or evil. An automobile is not evil. A new car is not evil. The *best model* of a new car is not evil. But the cheapest used car may be flagrantly evil for the Christian already staggered by debts and stingy about his giving to God. The world system leaves God out; thus any purchase that leaves God out is a flirtation with the world system. Logic: "It was such a good deal"; rationalization: "But it was on sale" are not justifications for buying anything or spending any money outside of the will of God.

Thus a doctrine of how to buy and prove our love for God in any economic situation is basically this: (1) Learn contentment in the will of God in every circumstance of life; and (2) love God more than any "thing" either possessed or desired. When prosperity comes as it has for many believers, the spiritual Christian will use it to give more (in proportion, not merely in dollar amount), not necessarily to buy more.

Paul concludes this chapter of principles for personal finances with this reminder (and remember that these words do not apply just to those who are in a higher income bracket—they apply to most Christians today): "Charge them that are rich in this world, that they be not high-minded, nor trust in uncertain riches, but in the living God, who giveth us richly all things to enjoy; that they do good, that they be rich in good works, ready to distribute, willing to communicate; laying up in store for themselves a good foundation against the time to come, that they may lay hold on eternal life" (I Tim. 6:17-19).

A spiritual Christian will practice full giving in full employment, inflated giving in an inflated economy, and careful buying at all times. And by his use of all his money he will prove or disprove his love for God.

9

USING YOUR GIFTS

ONE OF THE PRINCIPAL USES of the word *spiritual* is to designate the spiritual gifts which God gives to His people (Rom. 1:11; I Cor. 12:1; 14:1). They are spiritual gifts because the Spirit bestows them, and their proper use is the responsibility of one who would live the spiritual life. And yet there are many believers who have no conception of the meaning of spiritual gifts, no inkling of what their gift might be, and no understanding of how gifts are used in service to others; consequently, they cannot live the spiritual life in its full expression. By contrast, the spiritual man will know and use his spiritual gifts.

WHAT IS A SPIRITUAL GIFT?

Although the Greek word for spiritual gift is used in a breadth of meaning in the New Testament, it usually refers to the special gifts or abilities given to men by God. With the exception of I Peter 4:10 the word is used in the New Testament only by Paul. There are three places where the subject is discussed in detail—Romans 12, I Corinthians 12, and Ephesians 4. A spiritual gift is a God-given ability for service. This simple definition incorporates the source of gifts (God-given), the meaning of gifts (abilities), and the purpose of gifts (service). If we keep in mind that a spiritual gift is primarily an ability, this will keep us from much of the confusion that exists in people's minds concerning this subject. Many think of a spiritual gift as an office in the church which only a privileged few can ever occupy. Or else they consider spiritual gifts so out of reach of the ordinary believer that the best he can hope for is that someday he might happen to discover some little gift and be allowed to exercise it in some small way. Both of these conceptions are wrong.

A spiritual gift is primarily an ability given to the individual. This means that the gift is not a place of service, for the gift is the

ability, not where that ability is exercised. The gift of pastor, for instance, is usually associated with the office or position a person may occupy in the pastorate. But the gift is the ability to give shepherd-like care to people, regardless of where this is done. Of course, the man who occupies the office of a pastor should have and exercise the gift of pastor, but so should a dean of men in a Christian school. Indeed (though this may seem shocking at first), why shouldn't a Christian woman be given the gift of pastor to use among the children in her neighborhood or in her Sunday school class or as a dean of women? Now I did not say that women should become pastors of churches to do the preaching and take the leadership of the people. I think that the office or position of the pastorate is reserved for men only; but this does not mean that the gift or the ability cannot be given to women. Have you not ever known a woman who has so ministered as a church visitor for a congregation (and often on the payroll of the church)?

Another good example which highlights the difference between the gift and the place where it is exercised is the gift of teaching. Most of us connect the gift of teaching with the formal classroom situation. It certainly ought to be exercised there, but it may be used under many other circumstances as well. Is not the dear lady exercising the gift of teaching who patiently and willingly leads the Bible club that my children attend each week in the garage of a friend's home? This is not a formal school situation, but a great deal of teaching goes on in that place. Indeed, the Scriptures exhort that the older women "teach the young women to be sober, to love their husbands, to love their children" (Titus 2:4). Here is teaching done on a personal basis. The gift is the ability, not the place where that ability is used. What benefit would come to the church of Christ if every member would realize that he could use spiritual gifts all the time and under many different circumstances.

A spiritual gift is not primarily a place of service; neither is it a particular age group ministry. Frequently one hears someone say that he has the gift of young people's work. Actually there is no such gift (just as there is no gift of old people's work—a spiritual gift I have never heard anyone claim to have!). Actually the various age groups are the recipients of the exercise of gifts. To

be sure there are specialized techniques for the different age groups, but the spiritual gift is the basic God-given ability which is channeled through various techniques to others. There are also numerous methods which may be used in the exercise of gifts, but these methods are not the gifts themselves. For instance, writing is a method, but teaching and exhortation are the gifts which may be used either in an oral or written ministry. Thus the spiritual gift is the ability itself and not the place or method in or by which the ability is exercised.

Perhaps an illustration will help to clarify what a spiritual gift is. I knew a man who obviously had the gift of working with his hands. He could make anything. In his home was a beautiful paneled den which he had done with his own hands. Refinishing or restoring furniture was no problem to him. However, doing this sort of thing was not his profession in life. He was a dentist. And he was a good one, for the same ability which showed itself all through his home made gold inlays that fit in your teeth. What was his gift? Not dentistry (that was his position or office), nor woodworking or goldworking (those were means he used). It was the ability to work with his hands. Likewise, spiritual gifts are not the positions we hold in the church nor the methods we use; they are the basic God-given abilities for service.

WHAT ARE THE SPIRITUAL GIFTS?

The Bible lists more than a dozen specific spiritual gifts. The spiritual gifts which are specifically listed in the Bible (not all of which are necessarily given in every generation) are the following: apostleship, prophecy, miracles, tongues, evangelism, pastor, ministering, teaching, faith, exhortation, discerning spirits, showing mercy, giving and administration. Romans 12, I Corinthians 12 and Ephesians 4 give the principal teaching on this in the New Testament. Three of the gifts, however, probably all Christians could have and use if they would. They are ministering, giving and showing mercy (Rom. 12:7-8). Ministering means serving; in I Corinthians 12:28 this same gift is called "helps." It is the basic ability to help other people, and there is no reason why every Christian cannot have and use this gift. Indeed, a spiritual Christian must. Showing mercy is akin to the gift of ministering and involves succoring those who are sick or afflicted. "Pure re-

ligion and undefiled before God and the Father is this, To visit the fatherless and widows in their affliction . . ." (James 1:27). Not all will be given equal opportunities to do this, but without this kind of activity there can be no true spirituality. Giving is the ability to distribute one's own money to others, and it is to be done with simplicity which means with no thought of return or gain for oneself in any way. We have already seen in the preceding chapter how giving proves one's spirituality or lack of it in the sight of God.

It is probably true to say, then, that every believer can have more than one spiritual gift. Unless disobedience is present, all could, it seems, have three gifts to use in the service of God. Many will have more in varying combinations within their lives. Gifts may come to light for use at different times in a believer's life, but certainly a spiritual Christian will be using whatever combination of gifts is his for the glory of God. Service apart from the use of spiritual gifts is not spiritual service; it is only a manifestation of the activity of self.

THE DEVELOPMENT OF SPIRITUAL GIFTS

Although it is God who gives us spiritual gifts, and although it is the Spirit who empowers us for the use of them, the believer himself may have a part in the development of his spiritual gifts. Even the most sacrificial dedication will not necessarily guarantee the best use of the spiritual gifts which one has. Yieldedness cannot make up for lack of proper development of gifts, though proper development can never take place without yieldedness.

The Bible gives two guidelines for the proper development of spiritual gifts. The first is expressed this way: "But covet earnestly the best gifts" (I Cor. 12:31). Here is obviously an instance in which the word *covet* is not used in a bad sense. The basic meaning of the word is "be zealous for" which can be directed toward good or evil ends. In this verse it means an ardent pursuit of the better gifts. Those better gifts have just been cataloged by Paul in verse 28 where he gives an order of priority to some of the spiritual gifts.

How can one ardently pursue the best gifts? It is certainly not a matter of sitting down and conjuring up enough faith to be able to receive them like lightning from heaven. Indeed the word

but that opens the verse indicates that we have a part to play
in this.

> Ver. 31a corrects the inference which an indolent nature
> or weak judgment might draw from vv. 29 f., supposing
> that God's sovereign ordination supersedes man's effort.
> Our striving has a part to play, along with God's bestow-
> ment, in spiritual acquisitions; hence the contrastive *but*.[1]

In some circles, of course, it is anathema even to suggest that man
has any part in a matter like this. It is entirely God's work, we
are told. But how else can this verse be interpreted? Coveting
the best gifts is a matter of diligent self-preparation so as to be
able to present to the Lord the very best faculties to be used in
the exercise of the spiritual gifts which He gives. For instance,
if one covets the gift of teaching which is third in Paul's priority
list, he undoubtedly will have to spend many years developing
that gift. A Bible teacher who knows the original languages of
the Scriptures will be a better teacher than one who does not
know them (all other factors being equal). But learning Greek
and Hebrew is not a matter of faith; it requires a great deal of
hard work. A good teacher will also know the best techniques
for communicating the truth. To be sure, these may be learned
from experience, but even this method requires disciplined self-
preparation just as does the more formal classroom method.

It seems to me that coveting even the very basic gift of helps,
which is also mentioned in this passage in Paul's priority list
(and which is a gift every believer can have), requires diligent
self-preparation. This is what I mean. A lot of people will never
be able to use the gift of helps simply because they do not have
time to do things for others because they are so occupied with
their own affairs. And yet the real reason is not lack of time—it
is lack of discipline which would enable them to make and keep
to a schedule that would not only give them time for others but
would also allow them to take adequate care of their own affairs.
In this example it is the discipline of a schedule which is necessary
in ardently pursuing the better gift of helps.

This is the first guideline for developing spiritual gifts. The
spiritual Christian will certainly be asking the Lord frequently if

1. G. G. Findlay, "The First Epistle of Paul to the Corinthians," *Exposi-
tor's Greek Testament*, II, 896.

he is doing all that he can to develop the gifts God has given him.

The second guideline is this: Be attentive to the ministry of others. When Paul expressed his desire to go to Rome to see the believers there he said that one of his purposes was "that I may impart unto you some spiritual gift, to the end ye may be established" (Rom. 1:11). What Paul evidently wished to do for the Romans was to deepen and further their comprehension of the purposes of God through the exercise of his gift of teaching. It was not that Paul could *bestow* spiritual gifts, but he could *impart the benefit* of his spiritual gifts. But, of course, if the full benefit was to be received by the Roman Christians they would have to be attentive to the apostle's ministry. No benefit would come to a believer, for instance, who was at home when Paul was ministering in the congregation. Less benefit would come to another who happened to be present in the meeting but whose mind was wandering while Paul spoke. These very simple matters—lack of attendance and lack of attention—are still reasons today why some never develop fully their spiritual gifts. God has given gifted men to the church "for the perfecting of the saints, for the work of the ministry, for the edifying of the body of Christ" (Eph. 4:12). This process should be a never ending cycle. Gifted people minister to others who are thereby developed so that they in turn can minister to others who are thereby built up so that they can exercise their developed gifts on others who in turn . . . . We are the only ones who can break that cycle either by not using or by not developing fully the gifts God has graciously bestowed on us.

Thus this second guideline tells us that no Christian, not even the most spiritual one, gets beyond the point where he cannot benefit from the exercise of the gifts of others. These are the guides for the development of spiritual gifts.

How Can I Discover My Gifts?

This of course is the question everyone wants an answer to, and it is not an easy question to answer. Nevertheless, three suggestions may help resolve it.

The first is this: *Be informed.* In other words, know what spiritual gifts there are. It is possible that you may discover that

you have a gift or two already. Some who read these pages have probably been taught that every believer has only one gift, but now you have learned that there are possibly three gifts which you may have and use. Others may not have known that showing kindness to others was a spiritual gift.

A former colleague of mine used to tell an amusing story on himself. He and his wife wanted very much to see a spectacular view from a certain very expensive resort hotel. But since they lived on a strict budget they decided that the only way they could ever do this was to go to the hotel for breakfast which would be the least expensive of the three meals. This they did, and furthermore they ordered the cheapest breakfast on the menu. However, when my friend went to pay the bill he was charged what seemed to him an exorbitant price for pancakes. They had both wondered why the menu had not given prices for any of the meals but they assured themselves that pancakes would certainly be one of the lowest priced breakfasts. And now to their chagrin they discovered that even pancakes were very expensive. And then the truth came to them. This was a *table d'hote*, not an *a la carte*, menu, and they could have had any breakfast or all of them for the same price as their pancakes. But then it was too late to enjoy the full satisfaction of what had been offered them. So it is with far too many Christians. They do not know or they sometimes do not want to know all that God could give them by way of spiritual gifts. So, be fully informed.

The second is this: *Be willing.* If we are unwilling in any area then God may not be able to let us use some gift; and conversely, if we are completely willing to do anything or go anywhere, the Lord may bring to light gifts which we never dreamed we had. I remember asking a seminary senior one day what he planned to do after graduation. He replied that he believed he had the gift of teaching and asked me if I knew of any opening in this field.

I told him that I did and that it was in a place where he could immediately begin teaching in English. I had in mind a teaching post on another continent but in a place where he could begin his ministry in English while he was learning a second language. But when I replied as I did he immediately became suspicious, and he quickly informed me that he did not feel called to the mission field. I simply asked him what difference that made.

After all, did he not feel called to teach? So what difference did it make where he did it? But he was not willing even to consider anything beyond the shores of the continental United States, so he did not pursue the opening which I had suggested. As a result, he has never been in a teaching situation in all the years of his ministry. I cannot help but feel that his unwillingness limited the Lord as far as using the gift of teaching was concerned.

One does not need such a dramatic example to illustrate this point. There are many ordinary laymen and women who miss the full use of their gifts simply because they will not tie themselves down to a regular Sunday school class or even to a simple administrative job in the church. We must be completely and unreservedly willing to do anything if we would know the fullest use of our spiritual gifts.

The third suggestion is this: *Be active.* The exercise of one gift may lead to the discovery of other gifts. For example, what gift did Philip have? When we are first introduced to him in the book of Acts we find him exercising the gift of serving (6:5). Call him a deacon if you wish (though it seems improbable that the office was established at this time), but what he did was to distribute the relief money to a group of bickering women, and that is no exalted job. But apparently he did it faithfully, and having proved himself in the difficult and menial task, the Lord brought to light in his life the added gift of evangelism (8:5). Suppose that Philip had said to the apostles that he did not feel called to serving widows. He might never have been allowed to evangelize the Samaritans. Faithful activity in the one area led to the discovery of a gift in another area.

Actually this first gift we have any record of Philip using was that basic gift of serving, helping or ministering. Does this not give us a clue for our own lives? Instead of waiting to discover what spiritual gifts we may have been given, why not simply begin to exercise the gift of helps or the gift of showing mercy or even the gift of giving? While we are faithfully using these basic gifts perhaps God will bring to light others in our lives.

This is the doctrine of spiritual gifts. The spiritual Christian will serve God through fully exercising his developed gifts. This kind of activity is one of the prime responsibilities of the spiritual life.

10

ROUTINE FAITHFULNESS

Too often messages on the spiritual life focus on crisis experiences in the believer's life. The exhortations of such messages normally call for some crisis decision. If a Christian hears such sermons year after year, either he becomes insensitive to the constant ringing of the alarm bell or he associates spirituality only with crisis situations. Admittedly we often need calls to decision and certainly spiritual principles should be applied in the crises of life. But it is equally true that since most of our time is spent in the routines of life we ought to apply spirituality in these areas as well.

The basis for Christians' judgment is faithfulness, and that is why "it is required in stewards, that a man be found faithful" (I Cor. 4:2). It is also true that most Christians' activities are comprised of routine affairs. Therefore, it is mostly in the area of the routines of life that faithfulness is required. Have you ever noticed that when Paul summarized the Christian's conduct he related it to the ordinary activities of life: "Whether therefore ye eat, or drink, or whatsoever ye do, do all to the glory of God" (I Cor. 10:31). It would be almost unnecessary for him to have said something like this: "Whether therefore ye pray or witness, do these things to the glory of God." We are more naturally thinking of the glory of God in these matters than in eating and drinking. Thus it is the routines of life (as well as the crises) in which a spiritual person will exhibit faithfulness to his Lord. And these are often the most difficult areas.

Not only is the area of the routine a problem for spiritual living, but consistency of practice is also a problem. There are few who cannot gird themselves for the unusual. Most can produce when pressed. This is also true in spiritual matters. If we are called

on to lead in public prayer or if we are asked to participate in some sort of campaign in relation to the Lord's work, or if we are backed to the wall concerning our faith, most of us can find whatever is necessary to come through in such situations. But we all tend to let our guard down in the routine. And if the same routine is our lot for very long we inevitably grow weary and often disheartened simply because the routine "gets us down." But if the Bible principles of spiritual living work at all, they certainly should work in the routines of life and they ought to work continuously.

God has an important word for this situation and a word that must be heeded if we are to live the spiritual life. What He has to say is bound up in a single word in the New Testament—a word which is translated in various ways but which means basically to lose heart. This is not a physical faintness or a mere laxness but more of a mental disinclination which may even at times approach cowardice. In the use of this word (and it is found only seven times in the New Testament) it is as if God puts His finger on basic areas of life to which we must give special attention lest we lose heart.

FAITHFULNESS IN PROBLEMS

"For which cause we faint not [do not lose heart]; but though our outward man perish, yet the inward man is renewed day by day" (II Cor. 4:16). Paul had had more than his share of problems when he wrote these words. Just in connection with his ministry to the Corinthians he had suffered a great deal. When he first went into the city the Jews had openly opposed him so much that he was ready to leave and go elsewhere. Only the appearance of the Lord in the night by a vision restrained Paul and kept him in Corinth for a year and a half (Acts 18:6-11). Even after this assurance from the Lord, he found himself hailed before Gallio's judgment seat, having been accused by the Jews. All of this was at the end of the second missionary journey. As the third journey began, Paul found himself at Ephesus, and he likened the problems he found there to fighting with wild beasts (I Cor. 15:32). In this city not only did the Jews oppose him but Gentile citizens of Ephesus were stirred up by the silversmiths to stage a gigantic protest meeting against the Christians. These

were some of the things in Paul's recent experience when he wrote II Corinthians 4:16.

If any man had a right to lose heart Paul certainly did in the face of such problems. But he said he would not do so for two reasons. First, anything is worth suffering for the sake of the ministry. If the grace of God can be seen through the lives of those who have been helped, then problems are a small thing to endure. Second, Paul assured himself with the promise that God renews the inward man daily even though the outward man is subject to all kinds of pressures and problems.

The example and teaching are clear. A spiritual person shows persistence, not faintheartedness, in the face of difficulties. He will not give up when the routine begins to grind to his very soul. Rather he will show consistent and persistent faithfulness to the task to which he has been called.

About six years later the Apostle Paul found himself in different circumstances. On appeal to Caesar he was confined under house arrest in Rome awaiting trial. Roman law decreed that in such cases the accused must wait trial until his accusers appeared. In case they chose not to press the case the prisoner must wait a full eighteen months before the case could be dropped. The Jews who accused Paul apparently chose to allow the case to go by default since Paul was in Rome this time two full years. Actually this was the wisest course of action for them; had they brought the matter to trial, no doubt Paul would have been acquitted and his ministry thus vindicated. But by not pressing charges they not only kept Paul out of circulation for two years but they also left a question mark over his ministry since he was neither acquitted nor found guilty. But in the meantime Paul had to be patient, and so did his circle of friends who were waiting it out with him. It is to these friends in Asia Minor that he wrote, "Wherefore I desire that ye faint not at my tribulations for you" (Eph. 3:13). He did not want them to be disheartened because of his predicament. Undoubtedly many were praying for his quick acquittal and release, and they needed patience and encouragement in the face of this problem. It would have been very easy and natural to grow discouraged as the months dragged on. How often have most of us said about a problem, "Oh, I wish it would just get settled one way or the other. I don't even

care if it goes against me—just so it gets settled. I can't stand this indecision any longer." Paul might well have said that, and so might his friends. But instead the exhortation to all of us is to be faithful in the face of unsettled problems, committing them to God and patiently awaiting His solution. This kind of faithfulness will certainly characterize the spiritual Christian.

FAITHFULNESS IN PRAYER

The second area in which we need to be faithful in the routine because we are all prone to faintheartedness is in our prayer life. Our Lord taught that men ought always to pray and not to lose heart. The audience who first heard these words were those to whom He had just spoken of His second coming (Luke 17:20 ff.), making this parable particularly applicable to those of us who are living on the very brink of the rapture of the church. Sometimes we who have this blessed hope in our hearts can be justly accused of becoming lazy in the Lord's work while awaiting His coming. This ought not to be; rather we should be the more zealous. And, of course, the most essential part of any Christian work is prayer.

The story of the parable is a study in contrasts. A widow, whose rights in that society would have been nil, is contrasted with an unjust judge (literally a judge of injustice) who apparently had to answer to no one. The wronged widow was seeking redress, and only because she kept coming to the judge did she receive what she requested. From this story the Lord draws three promises concerning prayer.

The first is that in contrast to the unjust judge who cared not at all for those who came before him we have a heavenly Father who cares infinitely for those who come to Him. The second is a corollary to the first: instead of position without any rights as was the widow's, we are God's elect with all of the privileges that such a relationship brings. We come to a heavenly Father as those who have been chosen by the Father to be the heirs of all things. Why, then, should we ever lose heart in prayer?

But we sometimes say God does not seem to hear our prayers, let alone answer them. The third promise answers this objection, for the Lord promises that He will "avenge them speedily." The words translated "speedily" do not rule out delay; they simply

mean quickly when the hour for the answer comes. The promise is not that the answer will come as soon as the request is made; the promise is that when the time arrives for the answer to be given, all the pieces of the puzzle will fall into place suddenly. The same expression is used in Revelation 1:1, the promise being that the events revealed in that book will all happen suddenly when they begin to occur. The promise is not that they will begin in John's lifetime. Likewise, delay in the answers to our prayers is not contradictory to the meaning of the promise that the vindication will come speedily. In the meantime we should never lose heart in praying, knowing that at God's correct time the answer will come suddenly.

The three promises, then, are that we have a heavenly Parent, a heavenly position and a heavenly promise. These are the encouragements to faithfulness in the routine of prayer. The spiritual Christian will not lose heart in prayer.

FAITHFULNESS IN GOOD WORKS

Have you ever known a person who is too spiritual to be any good? Sometimes you hear it said that he is so heavenly minded that he is no earthly good. The Lord puts His finger on this area by reminding us twice in the New Testament not to neglect good works (Gal. 6:9; II Thess. 3:13). In the Galatians reference the extent of these ordinary good deeds is delineated as "unto all men, especially unto them who are of the household of faith." This kind of goodness is an imitation of the life of Christ "who went about doing good" (Acts 10:38). In the Thessalonians reference the exhortation to good works is made in the face of contrary conduct on the part of some of the believers in that church. Some evidently had quit working under the guise of false piety in that they were waiting for the Lord to come. These people were not idle, but they were busybodies instead of busy persons. Apparently these believers were busily trying to convert others to the idea that they too should quit working in view of the nearness of the Lord's return (v. 11). This kind of pseudospiritual persuasion would have been very difficult to withstand, for it might seem as if the person was against promoting an expectant attitude toward the Lord's return. Paul exposed the nonsense

of such talk and encouraged those who were faithful in the routines of life that they were doing the right thing.

This area is one in which Christian workers have problems. It is very easy for one who is in full-time Christian work to justify his lack of time to do ordinary good works by his busyness in the Lord's work. The omission in such a line of thinking is simply this: ordinary good works are the Lord's work, and none of us, including full-time workers and spiritual Christians, should ever be disinclined to perform them.

FAITHFULNESS IN WITNESS

A life of doing good must be coupled with the direct and positive proclamation of the gospel (II Cor. 4:1). Doing good without witnessing the message is the social gospel; witnessing without doing good is the unadorned gospel. If we lose heart in this area, how tragic will be the results for others and how barren will be our own spiritual lives. There are two reasons stated in this verse for proclaiming the message at every opportunity. The first is the message itself. According to II Corinthians 3 it is a message of life, glory, righteousness, liberty and transforming power. The second reason is simply that we ourselves have experienced this transforming power, and since we know from our own experience what this gospel can do, we are impelled to tell others. We should never lose heart, because we know the *message* and because *we* know the message.

Bringing results (conversions) from the witness is something only God can do, but giving the witness is something we must do. Our Lord warned us that there would be many who would apparently receive the message but who would, after a time, prove by their failure to bring forth fruit that it had not been believed unto salvation (Luke 8:4-15). Paul warned us that in the last days there would be a great deal of so-called godliness but it would be the kind that showed no newness of life since it would be powerless (II Tim. 3:5). Nevertheless, our responsibility remains the same—sow the seed of the Word. One who loses heart in this area does not have a true and vital spiritual life.

These, then, are four areas of living in which we can demonstrate spirituality or lack of it every day. Knowing how to live triumphantly in the face of problems, being persistent in prayer

even when the coming of the answer is delayed, simply being good to people, and witnessing faithfully to the gospel of God's grace are the areas in which we can by faithfulness in the routine show the measure of our spirituality.

Or to put it another way (and I hope inoffensively), the emphasis of this teaching about not losing heart is simply this: it is more important to gird ourselves for the grind of life than it is to throw ourselves into high gear only for the grandiose affairs of life. The longer I live the more I am convinced that genuine spirituality is not really proved from the pulpit or classroom or Sunday school or board meetings; rather it is demonstrated best by consistent living before God first of all, and then before those closest to us in the home. A kind of spirituality can be seen on parade; the kind God wants is cultivated and practiced consistently and persistently in the routine of life.

PART III

SOME PRACTICAL
PROBLEMS

11

HOW CAN I KNOW IF I AM FILLED WITH THE SPIRIT?

THE FORMULA for spiritual victory is often expressed in terms of "Be filled with the Spirit"—and this is correct. Indeed, spirituality is being filled with the Spirit. But what does it mean to be filled with the Spirit? What would be the characteristics of a life that is Spirit-filled? Can a person know if he is filled with the Spirit? These questions, important as they are, are not easily answered; and when they are, the answers are usually not clear. But we must try to find clear answers from the Word, for the filling of the Spirit is basic to a balanced spiritual life.

WHAT IS THE FILLING OF THE SPIRIT?

As with most concepts, a clear definition is all-important not only to understanding the basic idea involved but also to guide in the ramifications drawn from it. The superstructure built on an idea is no better than the defining of it at the foundation.

The guideline for proper defining of Spirit-filling is found in Ephesians 5:18: "And be not drunk with wine, wherein is excess; but be filled with the Spirit." It is simply the *comparison* between drunkenness and Spirit-filling. This is not to deny that there is a sharp contrast between these two states in the verse, but it is to say that the comparison is what gives us the clue to a proper definition of the filling with the Spirit. And that basic clue is the idea of control. This is what we see in the comparison, for both the drunk and the spiritual person are controlled people—the one is controlled by the liquor he has consumed, and the other by the Spirit whom he has received. Under the influence and control of liquor a person acts and thinks in ways that are unnatural to him.

111

Similarly, a Christian who is controlled by the Spirit thinks and acts in ways that are unnatural to him. This is not to imply that his life will be erratic or abnormal, but it is to say that he will not be living a life which is governed by that which is natural to him, that is, his old nature. Thus to be filled with the Spirit is to be controlled by the Spirit.

Another fact about the filling of the Spirit which is also indicated in Ephesians 5:18 is that it is a repeated experience. The tense of the verb in the verse is present which suggests continuous action in contrast to a single action which is instantaneous. In other words, a Christian may be filled and filled and filled again. This was illustrated in the experience of the apostles during the early days of the church. On the day of Pentecost they were filled with the Spirit (Acts 2:4). A short time later, after a prayer meeting for boldness, the same group was filled again (Acts 4:31). It is interesting and important to notice that the apostles did not need to be filled this second time because some specific sin had come into their lives after the day of Pentecost. This second filling was necessary because they needed control of a new area (boldness) in the face of a new problem (the prohibition to speak by the Sanhedrin). In other words, repeated fillings may be necessary because new areas of life come to light which need to be brought under the control of the Spirit. Of course it is also true that a Christian needs to be filled again and again when sin (which is ego control) breaks the control of the Spirit.

There is yet another fact about the filling of the Spirit suggested in Ephesians 5:18. The filling of the Spirit is demanded of a Christian (the verb "be filled" is an imperative). Believers are expected to be Spirit-filled; they do not have a choice. Again the book of Acts illustrates this, for the filling is mentioned at least nine times there and always in connection with the desired or ideal state of the individual or of the church. And of course, the Spirit stands ready to do the same for the church today.

How Can One Be Filled with the Spirit?

The way to receive the filling of the Spirit is often associated with some sort of tarrying or pleading simply because the disciples were told to wait in Jerusalem for the day of Pentecost

(Acts 1:4). Actually tarrying and pleading are not prerequisites for filling. That for which they were told to tarry before the day of Pentecost was called by the Lord "the promise of the Father" and was further explained as the fulfillment of the promise to "be baptized with the Holy Ghost" (Acts 1:5). They tarried for the baptism of the Spirit, and that is what they received on the day of Pentecost—and the filling along with it (Acts 11:15-16; cf. 2:4).

It is this confusion between the baptism and the filling of the Holy Spirit that usually leads to wrong formulas for the filling of the Spirit.

Baptism	*Filling*
Occurs only once in each believer's life	Is a repeated experience
Never happened before day of Pentecost	Occurred in the Old Testament
True of all believers	Not necessarily experienced by all
Cannot be undone	Can be lost
Results in a POSITION	Results in POWER
Occurs when we believe in Christ	Occurs throughout the Christian life
No prerequisite (except faith in Christ)	Depends on yieldedness

While the book of Acts records instances of the baptism of the Spirit (on the day of Pentecost and in the house of Cornelius [Acts 1:5; 11:15-16]), the explanation of what happens when one is baptized is not given in Acts. Only in I Corinthians 12:13 is the meaning of the baptizing work of the Spirit explained; it is said to be that by which we are joined to the body of Christ. This is why we can say confidently that the baptism is something that occurs once (because no Christian, once joined to Christ, can ever be unjoined), that it happens when one is saved (otherwise there would be saved people who were not united to Christ), and that it is primarily a matter of position rather than power. All this is borne out by the explanatory verse, I Corinthians 12:13, in which the tense of the verb *baptized* is such as to indicate an accomplished event, in which "all" believers are included

(among them some who had not spoken in tongues [I Cor. 12: 30]), and in which the resulting position is clearly stated as a place in the body of Christ.

Furthermore, no tarrying is indicated anywhere in the New Testament after the day of Pentecost as a prerequisite for being baptized with the Spirit. The only other specified instance of baptism in Acts took place in the house of Cornelius (10:45; 11: 15-16), and it occurred there at the moment the people believed while Peter was in the midst of his message to them. The pattern for Gentiles coming into the body of Christ as laid down in the house of Cornelius included no praying, no pleading, no tarrying—only believing in Jesus Christ, in response to which God immediately baptized them with the Spirit. God continues to follow the same pattern today.

But what about the filling of the Spirit? What are the conditions for it? Again we search the pages of the New Testament in vain for an example of believers praying for the filling of the Spirit since the day of Pentecost. The nearest thing to such an example is Paul's prayer for the believers in Ephesus in Ephesians 1:17. Yet even this is not a prayer for the filling of the Spirit. Actually, there is no example of such, although most people think this is the way to be Spirit-filled.

Even though God does not require us either to tarry or to agonize in prayer for the filling of the Spirit, this does not mean that the filling is without conditions. In one word, the condition is obedience, and while prayer may be involved in meeting the demands of obedience, yieldedness is the prerequisite for filling. This is, of course, exactly what the idea of control implies, for since the Spirit does not force His control on our lives, we must yield to His control and that will result in being filled with or controlled by the Spirit.

Yieldedness includes both the initial, crisis, complete act of dedication (as discussed in chap. 7) and a daily walk in dependence on the power of the Spirit. This latter aspect is what is spoken of in Galatians 5:16: "This I say then, Walk in the Spirit, and ye shall not fulfill the lust of the flesh." Here the tense of the verb is present, indicating a continuous dependence on the Spirit. Actually walking is, by its very nature, a succession of dependent acts. When one foot is lifted in order to place it in front of the

other one, it is done so in faith that the foot remaining on the ground will support the full weight of the body. Each foot in turn acts as a support while the other foot is being moved forward. Walking can only be done successfully by successive acts of faith in the power of one's feet. Likewise the Christian walk can be done successfully only by constant dependence on the Holy Spirit's control over one's life.

To be Spirit-filled, then, is to be Spirit-controlled. And to be thus controlled requires the yieldedness of a dedicated life and of a daily dependence on the power of the Spirit. Prayer and human effort may be involved in meeting these conditions, but when met the control of the Spirit (and thus the filling) is automatic.

A very practical question arises at this point: Can you ever say that you are filled with the Spirit? If you have ever been in a meeting where the speaker has asked those who are filled with the Spirit to give some indication that they know this is so, you noticed that most were reluctant to do so. Is this hesitation right, or should one be able to know he is filled with the Spirit and not hold back in raising a hand to let it be known? Some leaders, feeling that there need be no hesitation, are urging God's people to (1) be yielded and (2) stand up and declare that they are now filled with the Spirit. Which is right—the reluctance which most of us seem to have, or the aggressive assertion which some want us to have?

In a certain sense both emphases are correct. It is true that when one yields to the control of the Spirit, He takes over and gives direction to the life. This is filling, and a person may be assured that he is controlled or filled as long as he has consciously yielded to the Spirit. Why, then, the hesitation? It is because we realize that none of us has arrived and that there will always be areas of life coming to light which will need to be brought under the control of the Spirit as life progresses. Walking is not arriving. Each step must be taken in dependence on Him, and with each step is the possibility of stumbling. People are hesitant, therefore, to raise their hands indicating that they know that they are filled with the Spirit simply because they realize, however vaguely or clearly, that tomorrow's problems and circumstances

will bring new tests of control which will have to be decided then.

Paul wrote of such certainty and uncertainty in the same verse. "For I know nothing . . . [against] myself; yet am I not hereby justified: but he that judgeth me is the Lord" (I Cor. 4:4). In relation to the filling of the Spirit, some need to be assured that they can experience His control; others need to be warned against overconfidence lest they feel there are no more battles of control to be won.

What Are the Characteristics of a Spirit-filled Life?

How can one know if he is filled with the Spirit? What will his life to be like? In what ways will Spirit-filled Christians be similar to other Christians, and how will they be different? The answers to these questions are important in order to have proper guidelines for the Spirit-filled life and to avoid setting up a subjective pattern which we force believers to conform to if they want to prove that they are Spirit-filled.

1. Christlikeness. Christlikeness is the primary manifestation of the filling of the Spirit. It is also a universal characteristic of it; that is, all who are Spirit-filled will show in their lives the features of Christlikeness. But what is Christlikeness? Undoubtedly most of us tend to mirror our concept of Christlikeness in our own personalities rather than seeking to change our personalities to conform to the biblical picture of Christlikeness. Extroverts inevitably think Christ was an aggressive, outgoing extrovert. Introverts can only picture Him as a meek and mild Man who never asserted Himself. The sharp, Christian businessman probably thinks Christ would have been a millionaire had He chosen to be in business; while the ordinary, timid believer is equally sure that the Lord would have as little as possible to do with business, stock markets, and all things financial. Inevitably, we tend to project ourselves into our concept of Christlikeness.

What is genuine Christlikeness? Whatever it may or may not involve, most agree that it is the fruit of the Spirit; and this, as far as Galatians 5:22-23 is concerned, involves nine characteristics. If the Spirit controls one's life, then the fruit of the Spirit will be displayed, and this is Christlikeness. But the fruit of the Spirit

is too often understood in a very superficial way which yields a defective concept of Christlikeness.

What really is meant by the nine features of the fruit of the Spirit? What, for instance, is love? Certainly it is not some sort of spineless sentimentality. Love is doing the will of God, and this may involve all kinds of differing actions. Our Lord who, as God, is love could not, for instance, have been doing something unloving when He forcibly drove the money changers out of the temple. Love may at times cover sin by choosing not to expose it, but it never condones sin. Christlikeness involves a basic love of doing the will of God which could, in a given instance, be demonstrated in an act which on the surface seems to be unkind.

Likewise joy is something which does not depend on surface circumstances but which in the Scriptures is related basically to seeing other believers advance in the knowledge of the truth (III John 4; Phil. 2:2; I Thess. 2:19). In other words, Christlike joy comes from having an effective ministry with other people, just as Christ did (Heb. 12:2).

Peace is the tranquility which only a believer can know because he is in a right relation to God (Rom. 5:1; Eph. 2:17). It does not come from earthly security which possessions are sometimes thought to bring (Matt. 8:20). Peace with God can be experienced even in the midst of the greatest disharmony in other earthly relationships (Matt. 10:34), for it is based primarily on our vertical relationship with the Lord. To be sure, there will be horizontal ramifications, but the Bible warns that it will not always be possible to live at peace with all men (Rom. 12:18).

Long-suffering is the evenness in one's character and conduct which causes him never to display a desire for revenge. It includes the trait of patience but also the positive restraint that works with people to advance the glory of God in them. It may include prodding someone (John 14:9) but always with the goal of promoting his growth in grace.

Gentleness and goodness are two sides of the same coin. The first means beneficent thoughts, and the other means kind actions. Obviously our Lord was always Christlike, so even His act of destroying a herd of swine could not have been contrary to goodness.

Faithfulness means serving and living with regularity and buy-

ing up all the opportunities God gives us. It involves the routine of working, worshiping, witnessing. Of course it includes the crises of life, but for all of us faithfulness is largely a matter of godliness in the grind of life. Our Lord exhibited this in circumstances He must have chafed under (Luke 2:52; 4:39; Heb. 5:8), and this fruit of the Spirit is required of all believers (I Cor. 4:2).

Meekness is gentlemanliness. It is not weakness (notice the way our Lord dealt with His opponents in Matt. 15). Of Moses, the great leader, it was said that he was the meekest man in all the earth (Num. 12:3). In our day leadership is too often built on a dynamic personality or personal magnetism; biblical greatness is based on meekness.

Self-control is the discipline of all areas of life, especially the area of morality. It means bringing all facets into disciplined subjection so that the life can be as finely honed as possible to do the will of God. It certainly means no laziness, no sloppiness, no aimlessness, no self-indulgence.

All of these nine features together make up the fruit of the Spirit. The fact that these are the fruit, not fruits, of the Spirit reminds us that all nine must be present at the same time, completely integrated and acting on each other and producing a balanced, Spirit-controlled and fruitful life.

A practical question arises at this point. Let me illustrate it this way. I have heard many testimonies from new students that go something like this: "When I first same to school I went to Dr. So-and-so's class, and I admired him so. I thought that I wanted to be just like him. Then I went to Professor So-and-so's class, and he so captivated me that I knew I had to be just like him. This continued through all my classes, and each professor seemed to be just the one I wanted to model my life after. But pretty soon I became frustrated because I realized I couldn't be like them all, so finally I realized that God wanted me to be the best representative of me that I could be. And that's what I'm trying to be." Of course the obvious error in that conclusion is that God wants me to be the best representative of *Christ* that I can be. And yet, having said that, I realize that this isn't the whole story because there are God-given differences between you and me. So the practical problem Christlikeness raises is this: If

all believers were Christlike, in what ways would we all be similar and in what ways different?

The answer lies in the interrelation between Christlikeness, natural gifts, spiritual gifts and personality. Differences in natural endowments including personality traits are part of all of us. Some of these differences are amoral; that is, they are neither bad nor good of themselves. But some are due to the sin nature and the extent to which it is controlled or unleashed. As believers we are further endowed with spiritual gifts in different combinations for each of us. The old nature in a believer is not eradicated, and it may continue to express its characteristics in one's life. Natural differences are not necessarily erased when we become Christians. And yet Christlikeness is an absolute which is not different for each believer. All are to exhibit the kind of character and conduct which the fruit of the Spirit produces. All are to manifest the fruit of the Spirit, but each will do it through his own different personality and with his particular gifts. There will be differences because of endowments; there should be similarity because of Spirit-control. There must never be excuses because of unwillingness to allow the Lord to effect changes in our personalities or because we allow the sin nature to take over.

To be specific, the believer with a low IQ should exhibit love, joy, peace, etc.; and the believer with a high IQ should do likewise in his sphere of activity. The believer with lesser gifts should exercise them so that he bears the fruit of the Spirit; likewise, the believer with greater gifts. An extrovert who runs over others just because of his overpowering personality should seek to let the Spirit change him and produce meekness in him. The lazy Christian must never excuse his defect as constitutional but should let the Spirit bear the fruit of discipline in his life. The Christlike character and conduct of Christians should be similar; the God-given and amoral distinctions in us make us different; and sinful differences must never be tolerated. I am to be the best representative of myself that I can be and that the Lord can make me to be, as long as that representation manifests Christlikeness in the conduct of my particular God-given qualities of life. This kind of life is one that is controlled by and filled with the Spirit.

2. A life of service. "In the last day, that great day of the feast, Jesus stood and cried, saying, If any man thirst, let him come unto me, and drink. He that believeth on me, as the scripture hath said, out of his belly shall flow rivers of living water. (But this spake he of the Spirit, which they that believe on him should receive: for the Holy Ghost was not yet given; because that Jesus was not yet glorified)" (John 7:37-39). During the preceding seven days of the Feast of Tabernacles, libations of water which had been brought from the Pool of Siloam had been made at the time of the morning sacrifice. On the eighth day, when our Lord spoke these words, apparently no libations were offered, which made His claim to be the One who could satisfy all the more striking. But He not only said that He could satisfy; in addition He predicted that the Holy Spirit will overflow in the life of the believer, spreading the blessing he has received. But, of course, the Spirit must be allowed to do this by being given control over the believer's life.

What kind of service will the Spirit-filled believer be doing? The answer in general is that he will be exercising in the power of the Spirit his particular combination of spiritual gifts. But there is a more specific answer than this, and it comes from an interesting accompaniment of Spirit-filling in the book of Acts. Notice the instances where the filling is mentioned and what happened thereafter.

The filling on the day of Pentecost (Acts 2:4) was followed by the conversion of three thousand people (2:41). Peter was filled again as he spoke to the Sanhedrin (4:8). After that group warned him not to preach Jesus anymore, the disciples, on hearing the report, prayed for boldness to do what they had been warned not to do. Again they were filled with the Spirit (4:31) and people continued to be saved (5:14). The choosing of the seven to help the apostles in chapter 6 (a qualification for those chosen was to be filled with the Spirit [v. 3]) resulted in a large number of priests turning to the Lord (6:7). From the death of Stephen, who was one of that group of seven, came the conversion of the Apostle Paul (8:1; cf. 9:5). At the beginning of his new life in Christ Paul was filled with the Spirit (9:17), and the fruit of his life is well known (cf. 13:9). The record of the filling

in the life of Barnabas is followed in the same verse by "much people was added unto the Lord" (11:24).

In every instance of the filling of the Spirit in the book of Acts the filling of the Spirit, controlling the disciples in their service for their Lord, resulted in the salvation of souls. This link between filling and soul-winning ought to be more direct in most believers' lives. It was true in the early church, and it remains a manifestation of the filling today. To be sure there are indirect and equally vital links as well. It undoubtedly required in the early church many helping in the work to accomplish the spectacular results recorded in Acts. Those who prayed (4:24) had a part in winning others, and certainly those who gave of their possessions so that there would be no financial lack (4:34) were an important link in bringing many to Christ. But the church, each one exercising his particular gifts under the control of the Spirit, saw souls saved as its people were filled with the Spirit. We must conclude, then, that Christian service that results in people coming to Christ is a characteristic of the Spirit-filled life.

3. Praise, worship, thanksgiving and submissiveness. The classic verse on the filling of the Spirit in Ephesians 5:18 is followed by a list of four characteristics of that kind of life. The first is the outward expression of praise through "speaking to one another in psalms and hymns and spiritual songs." The second is an inner attitude of worship evidenced by "singing and making melody in your heart to the Lord." The third is "giving thanks always for all things." This expression is as inclusive as possible, and it was written by a man who was at the time under house arrest in Rome. The fourth is submissiveness to one another which will affect all the relationships of life, so that peace and harmony will reign between husbands and wives, parents and children, employers and employees.

Each of these characteristics of the Spirit-filled life becomes a test for determining if you are filled with the Spirit. No inner joy and no outward expression of it in singing and testimony means no control by the Spirit. A complaining attitude comes from self, not the Spirit who wants to make us thankful always. And disharmony at home or at work is not of the Lord, but of self. At this point we are right back where we started from, for at the very first I said that spirituality is best demonstrated in the home.

How can I know if I am filled with the Spirit? The simplest answer is a single test: have I to the best of my knowledge and ability given the control of my life to Him? If the answer is yes, then you are filled. But this does not mean it will last even for a day. For tomorrow another problem or a new circumstance may arise in which you will take control and in that area you will not be filled with the Spirit.

The basic test is that of control; the corroborating evidences of Spirit-filling are the characteristics just discussed. If Christlikeness is developing (it will never be perfectly or fully developed in this life), if your life is given to soul-winning service, and if praise, worship, thanksgiving and submissiveness are in your heart and actions, then the Spirit is in control. You need not look for some startling manifestation of Spirit-filling, nor need you plead for some ecstatic experience. Yield control to God; keep it there, and use all the powers available to develop the biblical characteristics of the Spirit-filled life.

12

THE WILES OF THE DEVIL

ACCORDING TO THE DICTIONARY, a wile is "a trick or stratagem, a sly artifice, deceit." The wiles of Satan are a major concern for the Christian who would live a spiritual life. And yet, as in other areas of the spiritual life, this too is a matter which needs balance. There are some believers who see Satan at work in every detail of life; others fail to recognize his activity at all. Some, strange to say, actually or at least practically deny his real existence. Apparently there are those who feel that Satan merely exists in the mind of man; therefore, the fact that we think he exists is the only genuine existence he has. However, the Scriptures teach that Satan was alive before man was ever created; thus he existed before there was a human mind to conceive of or recognize his existence (Ezek. 28:13-15). Furthermore, every reference by our Lord to the evil one is a proof of his real existence (Matt. 13:39; 25:41; Luke 10:18; John 12:31; 16:11), or else one is forced to conclude that Christ did not know what He was talking about. Of course, modern theology explains these references as Christ accommodating Himself to the ignorance of the people of His day; but such accommodation, if it were so, would invalidate His entire message. Satan exists. The Bible and our Lord attest to that fact.

But—getting back to the wiles or tricks of Satan—how can Satan be so clever? There are at least three factors that contribute to his mastery of the art of trickery. For one thing, he belongs to an order of creatures that is higher than man (Heb. 2:7). He is an angel, though fallen now, and among the angels he was a cherub (Ezek. 28:14). This would seem to give Satan a constitutional superiority over man.

123

For another thing, Satan's experience is far greater than any man's could ever be. By his very longevity Satan has acquired a breadth and depth of experience which he matches against the limited knowledge of man. He has observed other believers in every conceivable situation, thus enabling him to predict with accuracy how we will respond to circumstances. Although Satan is not omniscient, his wide experience and observation of man throughout his entire history on earth give him knowledge which is far superior to anything any man could have. Apparently, too, Satan knows the Bible; therefore, a believer has no particular advantage over him in this area either.

A third advantage Satan has is his ability to transform himself in a variety of ways. These vary all the way from presenting himself as an angel of light and his ministers as ministers of righteousness (II Cor. 11:14-15) to showing himself as a dragon with horns and a tail (Rev. 12:3). Although this latter representation is often said not to be in the Bible, it is; and it is there to help us realize the fierceness of Satan's nature as he engages in a death struggle with God's people.

To sum up: Satan because of his constitutional superiority, his great knowledge, and his chameleon character is a foe whose wiles are not to be taken lightly by any Christian.

SATAN'S PLAN

From the time of his first sin until his final defeat, Satan's plan and purpose have been, are, and always will be to seek to establish a rival rule to God's kingdom. He is promoting a system of which he is the head and which stands in opposition to God and His rule in the universe.

But to carry forward this program, Satan uses a plan which is extremely deceptive because of its subtlety. Instead of promoting a kingdom whose charcteristics are exactly opposite to the features of God's rule, he seeks to counterfeit God's program in the world. Counterfeiting the will of God has been, presently is, and always will be his plan as long as he has freedom.

Of course, counterfeiting has a single purpose, and that is to create something as similar to the original as possible and to do it by means of a shortcut. If you were going to counterfeit dollar bills, you would be foolish to put Lincoln's picture on them, for

that would obviously show them up as counterfeit. You would place Washington's picture on them so as to make them as similar to the genuine article as possible. But you would take some shortcut—perhaps a less accurate and thus imperfect engraving —thus revealing your work as counterfeit to the experts. But in all features of their appearance, the bills would have to appear to be just the same as genuine ones.

Satan's plan is a counterfeit plan to God's, and this is the most important fact to know about all of his purposes in this world. If you grasp this, then you will be well on the way to a successful defense against him. If not, it will be all the more easy for him to deceive you. He is a master counterfeiter, and he is trying to promote something that is similar, not dissimilar, to the plan and will of God. Satan, with all of his intelligence and long experience, knows that if he puts something which is clearly evil in the path of a Christian, he is apt to be alert to the fact that this comes from Satan and as a consequence be on guard against it. But if Satan can offer something which though good in itself is not the best, he will be more likely to gain the victory over the believer.

Satan boldly announced this counterfeit policy when he first sinned. In Isaiah 14:14 it is recorded of him that he declared his opposition to God this way: "I will be like the most High." There is a counterfeit—like, not unlike, the Most High.

We have already examined how Satan pawned this off on Adam and Eve in the Garden of Eden in Genesis 3. He offered Eve the tantalizing prize of being like God, knowing good and evil, by enticing her to take something which was good for food, pleasant to the eyes, and productive of knowledge. It all seemed good, except that eating of that fruit was contrary to the revealed will of God.

At the temptation of Christ, Satan tried the same counterfeiting approach. The offer of food was not inherently evil. The suggestion that Christ cast Himself off the pinnacle of the temple without doing Himself harm would have brought Him (had He done it) recognition from the people which was entirely right that He have. To have the kingdoms of the world is His prerogative, and He will rule over them in a future day. Actually the items Satan offered Christ (sustenance, recognition and power) were not wrong in themselves nor were they things Christ should

not have had. What was wrong was the way Satan was tempting our Lord with these things; for he was trying to obtain these glories without the suffering involved, particularly the suffering of His death on the cross. The ends Satan offered were right and proper for Christ to have; but the means involved a shortcut, by-passing the cross. It was a clever counterfeit, and completely in line with Satan's usual method.

As we come to the end of this age, Satan through his demons is promoting false doctrine (I Tim. 4:1) with the purpose of producing in people a form of godliness but without the true power of God (II Tim. 3:5). Here is another counterfeit—a semblance of godliness, not ungodliness, but that which leaves out the power of God.

But doesn't Satan promote evil, too? Yes, he does. Ananias' and Sapphira's lying hypocrisy was induced by Satan (Acts 5:3), and infidelity is a temptation from Satan (I Cor. 7:5). And, of course, all of his "good" counterfeits are evil. The point to remember is that Satan will do anything and everything he can to detract from the will of God. Counterfeiting in the form of substituting something seemingly good for the plan of God is likely his preferred way of doing things, but he cannot always exercise his preference. So he will do anything he can and work against people in any way, at any point and on any level he can whether that means using evil or "good."

SATAN'S DEVICES

In carrying out his design to counterfeit the plan of God, Satan has many devices which he uses. Furthermore, he will employ them at any time and in any variety and combination of ways. But to be forewarned is to be forearmed.

1. We have already emphasized that Satan is the master counterfeiter. This is the device of deceit. Another example of this tactic is his sowing of tares among the wheat in this age (Matt. 13:24-30, 36-42). Tares are the plant known as the "bearded darnel" which in the blade is indistinguishable from wheat. Since tares are unsuitable as human food they must be separated from the wheat, which can be done with greater ease when the grain matures. Sowing tares in a field for purposes of revenge was a crime under the Roman government. In the parable, our Lord

likens the tares which Satan sows to children of the devil, while
the wheat symbolizes the children of God. In sowing the two
together in the field (which is the world), the devil today deceives many. People who are in reality tares may be deceived
into thinking they are wheat because they have made a profession
of Christianity and exhibit some of the characteristics of believers. This gives them a false sense of security. Undoubtedly
there are many tares sitting in church pews and serving on church
boards who do not realize that they are headed for "a furnace of
fire" where "there shall be wailing and gnashing of teeth" (Matt.
13:42). I often think that Satan is far more satisfied with unsaved people who are in church on Sunday morning than with
those who may be playing golf or sleeping off a hangover, for
they are more apt to think that they are all right, whereas those
not in church might have some sense or feeling that all is not well.
This is one of the ways Satan deceives the world.

2. Sometimes Satan employs open opposition to the work of
God in order to thwart its progress. There are several examples
of this in the Bible.

When Paul was in Corinth writing his first letter back to the
Thessalonians he expressed his desire to return to Thessalonica
to strengthen the young church; but, said he, "Satan hindered us"
(I Thess. 2:18). This hindrance apparently refers to the security,
or bail, which Jason had to guarantee and which involved an
agreement that Paul would not return to that city again and become a public nuisance (Acts 17:9). Paul saw this action on the
part of the rulers of Thessalonica as an action of Satan.

Sometime later, the risen Lord warned the church at Smyrna:
"The devil shall cast some of you into prison, that ye may be tried"
(Rev. 2:10). Here was open opposition instigated by Satan using
unbelievers to seize some of the believers and imprison them.

At the same time the church at Pergamum was said to dwell
"where Satan's seat [throne]" was (Rev. 2:13). This could refer
either to the worship of the Roman emperor, or to the worship of
Zeus at his magnificent altar on the Acropolis, or to the worship
of the Greek gods in the temple. Or, of course, Satan's throne
could be a reference to all three forms of pagan worship. The
point is that in this instance Satan's open opposition to the gospel
was in the form of false religion—a tactic which he is still using

today in the form of both antichristian religions and so-called "Christian" cults. The form of the ritual may be very beautiful, the standards may even be moral, but if the saving death of Jesus Christ is left out, it is a false, satanic system.

3. In promoting his ends, whether deceptively or openly, Satan often employs a systematic theology to appeal to the intellectual pride of man. The church at Thyatira was warned about accepting the deep teachings of Satan (Rev. 2:24). Apparently a false prophetess in that church (whose actual name may or may not have been Jezebel) was promoting immorality and idolatry (v. 20) by incorporating these sins within a doctrinal system which probably made them appear as not sinful. Paul warned that the last days will be characterized by "doctrines of devils" (I Tim. 4:1), which, oddly enough, will include teaching asceticism as a means of trying to please God and gain His favor. Abstention, rather than indulgence, will be part of the satanic systematic theology of the last days.

It has sometimes been said that more likely one will find Satan at work in a seminary than in a bar. Undoubtedly he will work wherever he sees opportunities, but perhaps he needs to be less concerned about the bar, where man's own lusts will automatically take over, than about the seminary, where he fights for the minds of men and, if successful, can poison the stream at its source.

4. One of the most frequently used devices of Satan is the applying of pressure on the believer in various ways. It may be pressure that arises from the inability to maintain a good course of action. This was true of some women who had embarked on a life of self-denial which proved to be too severe for them. In their failure they had followed Satan. The pressure of that life of self-denial was too great, and the embarrassment that would have resulted from admitting it too overwhelming; so they yielded to satanic pressure (I Tim. 5:14-15).

In another instance, Paul warned that Satan could easily turn the proper remorse of a sin-burdened conscience into an occasion of further sin (II Cor. 2:11). To prevent this the church needed not only to forgive but also to restore the brother who had confessed and turned from his sin. Otherwise Satan might be able to put the man under the pressure of continued self-accusation

which would lead him into more sin. Continued introspection can often be the opening wedge for additional satanic pressure on the believer.

These two examples show that pressures can come from personally stepping out of the will of God (I Tim. 5) or from others' not doing His will (II Cor. 2). Often Satan does not have to enter the picture early or even frequently, since we can be led astray of our own lusts or be involved in a circumstance not of our own making. Pride or covetousness will sometimes lead a believer to seek to acquire something which of itself is neither good nor bad. But to gain it may require extra work which may lead to the neglect of the family which in turn will bring pressures that Satan can use to defeat that Christian. Too, the circumstances of twentieth century life are so increasingly complex as to demand more and more guidance from the Lord so that an individual knows when to say yes and when to say no, so that he avoids exposing himself to pressure which Satan might use as a leverage against him. We may be sure of one thing—he will use every advantage we give him.

5. Others of his devices (some of which we shall look at later in more detail) include discouragement, sidetrack, temptation, stagnation and, of course, any ruse which would keep the believer from normal and proper maturity in the spiritual life.

THE BELIEVER'S DEFENSE

All too frequently people run to one of two extremes in their thinking about Satan and his attacks on the believer. Some become over-occupied with him and as a result see Satan actively and intimately concerned with every problem or situation that goes wrong in their lives. I heard recently of a young Christian athlete who, every time he missed a shot, felt that he was out of the will of God and under attack by Satan. With help like this Satan receives credit for many feats he really has nothing to do with. We need to remember that within our own beings is the capacity to initiate, promote and commit sin. Mix in the world with the sin nature and there are two enemies which are more than able to overpower the Christian without involving Satan. Overoccupation with Satan can also lead to morbid introspection in which not only every action but also every motive is minutely

examined in the light of Satan's possible connection. On the other hand, this undue concern with Satan can sometimes provide a person with unjustified excuses for his actions. "Oh, Satan did it" becomes an out for the person to relieve him of responsibility for committing sin. But, of course, Satan does it through the person, who is involved in the responsibility for the action, and not against his will.

In contrast to overoccupation with Satan, there is the opposite attitude which underestimates his activity in the believer's life. Undoubtedly Satan is pleased when he can promote such deception, for if the believer does not recognize the source of the problem as being Satan, he cannot attack it in the right way. The trend today to seek to explain everything in terms of natural phenomena has without doubt provided Satan with a mask under which to work. For instance, personal emotional difficulties, church problems, adverse circumstances are seldom attributed to Satan. Indeed, to do so almost seems foolish, but it may be more foolish not to do so!

Somewhere between these two extremes lies a proper balance, but achieving it is not always easy. We need to be alert to all of Satan's possible devices, for he is at work attacking, deceiving, counterfeiting and seeking to defeat the believer at every opportunity. Thank God we are not left defenseless. Provision has been made to meet his attacks.

1. In two places in the New Testament we are told that the Lord Jesus lives in heaven to make intercession for His children (Rom. 8:34; Heb. 7:25). Apparently this work of praying for us has two aspects: curative and preventive. The curative is necessary to sustain fellowship when we sin (I John 2:1); the preventive helps keep us from sinning, particularly when attacked by Satan. The Lord gave us an insight into this in a petition He made just before His crucifixion when He said to the Father, "I pray not that thou shouldest take them out of the world, but that thou shouldest keep them from the evil" (John 17:15). The word *evil* as it appears in this verse can be either neuter (evil things) or masculine (evil one—Satan). The latter is the meaning John seems to prefer in his writings (cf. I John 2:13-14; 3:12; 5:18-19). Thus Christ is asking the Father to keep believers from Satan. What this means in terms of sparing us from attacks of Satan we

cannot know fully this side of heaven, but there we may learn all that the intercessory work of our Lord has meant on our behalf in defeating our adversary. This, of course, is a defense which He does entirely for us; we have no part except to receive its benefits.

2. A second line of defense for the believer is to know that the purposes of God may on occasion include using Satan to teach a particular lesson. In such instances our defense is to learn the lesson God has for us even though He may be using Satan in the process of teaching it. That was, of course, what God did in the case of Job when He permitted Satan to be used to carry out His own purposes in Job's life. A similar thing happened in Paul's life (II Cor. 12:7-10) when the Lord sent a messenger of Satan to inflict some kind of "thorn in the flesh" on him in order to keep him from getting proud over the revelations God had given him. The lesson Paul learned was the sufficiency of God's grace. Reliance on that was the only way he could defeat Satan and submit to the will of God. Such involvement of the will of God, Satan and the believer at the same time is often inscrutable; yet it happens.

3. It is always of primary importance in defeating Satan to take the proper attitude in relation to him. Though we have the power of God on our side, it is never wise to assume that victory is automatically guaranteed. To remember that we are engaging a mighty foe, the greatest of all of God's creatures, is to assume a proper attitude toward Satan. The example of this is recorded in Jude 9 where we are reminded that even as great an angel as Michael the archangel did not dare take on Satan alone but called on the Lord to rebuke him. No Christian, then, should ever feel that he is wise enough or powerful enough to engage Satan apart from complete dependence on the Lord.

4. A definite stand against Satan on the part of the believer is essential for victory. Why say this? Is it not self-evident? Yes, it is, but many Christians will never realize victory over the devil simply because they have never decided to take a stand against him. They are still flirting with the sin or temptation Satan puts in their path. They may even pray earnestly for victory and piously speak of their desire for relief, but in their hearts is still the desire to indulge and yield if only occasionally to some pet sin.

Only a definite decision to take decisive stand against the wicked one can ever put them on the road to victory.

James wrote of this, using a verb tense that means to take a decisive stand, when he said, "Resist the devil, and he will flee from you" (4:7). Likewise, the believer's armor is given in order that he might take a stand against his adversary (Eph. 6:11, 13-14). Such a stand is vital as a base of operations on which to wage the continual warfare that comes; without it there can be only retreat and defeat. With it there can be victory, though not without continued warfare.

5. A rather simple and concise formula for defeating Satan is given in Revelation 12:11: "And they overcame him by the blood of the Lamb, and by the word of their testimony; and they loved not their lives unto the death." There are three elements in the formula. The first, the basis of all victory over Satan, is the blood of the Lamb. This is not some mystical or even magical application of nearly literal blood today as the believer "claims" it or "dips" into its reservoir. The blood of the Lamb was shed on a hill outside Jerusalem, and that became the clear evidence of death having occurred. The blood is not in heaven; the crucified Christ is, and as such He has defeated Satan (Col. 2:15). And His victory makes our victory possible. This is what is meant by overcoming Satan by the blood of the Lamb.

The second element in the formula is something we can do to make Christ's victory applicable in our lives—be positive and consistent in our testimony for the Lord. It is a fatal mistake to believe that while faith in the death of Christ is required, testimony for Christ is optional. No testimony by both life and mouth means no defeat for Satan. The Lord reminded His disciples: "Ye are the light of the world. A city that is set on an hill cannot be hid. Neither do men light a candle, and put it under a bushel, but on a candlestick; and it giveth light unto all that are in the house" (Matt. 5:14-15). Like the candle under a bushel, a testimony hidden under cowardice, compromise, worldliness or indifferent neglect will be extinguished. Sometimes (and I hope I am not misunderstood in saying this) a defeated Christian does not need to pray more or read his Bible more—he needs to be out witnessing more.

The third feature of this formula for victory is a basic attitude

toward life itself—an attitude of self-sacrifice to the point of being perfectly willing to die for Christ. An attitude like this will put one's set of values in life in right perspective more quickly than anything else. Defeating Satan requires a martyr spirit. "Whosoever will save his life shall lose it; but whosoever shall lose his life for my sake and the gospel's, the same shall save it" (Mark 8:35).

6. Finally, victory over Satan requires the constant use of the armor which God has provided for the Christian (Eph. 6:11-18). This includes truth which, like a girdle, holds everything together and gives proper orientation to life. This, of course, is the truth of God, not the wisdom of men, and it needs to be the basis for how we look at everything. Finances and friendships, activities and attitudes, family and fun, science and psychology must all be governed by the truth of God as revealed in the Scriptures.

Righteousness is the breastplate to guard the vital organs of life. Is this the imputed righteousness we have by being in Christ? Of course. Is this the imparted righteousness which we live in daily life? Of course. Both are meant, for a righteous life has to be based on a righteous position, and a righteous position that does not manifest itself in godly living is probably not genuine.

Our feet should be prepared to do the will and work of God because we have experienced the peace of God which the gospel brings. No stumbling and no slowing down should characterize the believer.

Faith is the large shield that gives overall protection. This is not simply faith in the crises of life, but faith to overcome the tempter in the routine of life. We walk by faith and not by sight.

Around the head goes the helmet of salvation. How many Christians seem to feel that they need saving only from the neck down! We have already noticed that the dedicated life begins with the renewing of the mind (Rom. 12:2); our thought life needs to experience the effects of salvation.

The single offensive weapon is the sword of the Spirit which is the word of God. This is not simply the written Word, for the particular word used here and translated "word" means spoken word. The sword of the Spirit then, is the spoken proclamation of the written Word. It is not simply a New Testament carried

in one's pocket, however good that may be; rather, it is the spoken testimony which we give with our lips. The sword of the Spirit of Ephesians 6:17 is the word of testimony of Revelation 12:11.

The final feature of the armor is prayer, not just mouthings of petitions, but Spirit-guided prayer.

This is the armor provided for our protection, but God will not forcibly dress us in it. We have the responsibility to take it up (v. 13), and it will be a lifetime involvement. To be sure, we can put it all on in a moment, but developing skillful use of it requires a lifetime of practice. We may be sure too that Satan will seek to find the chinks in our armor in his unceasing and relentless fight against us.

Let me conclude this chapter on the wiles of the devil by reminding you of parts of three verses which a speaker paraphrased and put together for me many years ago, and which have been a source of real assurance: "Christ lives in me" (Gal. 2:20); "Greater is he that is in me, than he that is in the world" (I John 4:4); "He will never leave me, nor forsake me" (Heb. 13:5). Our Lord is our victory. Trust Him and use all the means He has provided to defeat the great enemy of our souls.

13

TEMPTATION

TEMPTATION IS COMMON TO MAN. Or as the Living New Testament expresses it: "But remember this—the wrong desires that come into your life aren't anything new and different. Many others have faced exactly the same problems before you" (I Cor. 10:13a). In fact, even the heroes of the biblical Hall of Fame experienced infamy. Remember Noah's drunkenness? Or Abraham's cowardice and lying before a heathen ruler? Or Moses' self-exaltation which made him strike the rock and kept him out of the promised land? Or Jacob's stratagems? Or the Patriarchs' mistreatment of Joseph? Or Elijah's murmuring? Or David's double sin? Or Hezekiah's ostentation? Or Jonah's rebellious spirit? Or Peter's denial of his Lord? Or John Mark's defection? Or Paul and Barnabas' strife? Some of the noblest men of the Bible have not only experienced temptation but have yielded to its power.

But to read or hear some on the spiritual life, one would think that the so-called victorious Christian never experiences temptation; or if he does, it is a slight and fleeting experience which really causes him no problem. I have just made a perusal of a half dozen books on the spiritual life. Only one of them mentioned temptation and then in only two paragraphs. Perhaps this unrealistic attitude toward the reality of temptation is the cause of discouragement among some believers who, thinking they have the "secret" of victory, suddenly find themselves not only confronted with temptation but actually overcome by it.

But, while temptation is common to man, the believer does not have to yield to it, for God in His mercy makes ways to escape so that we can bear it. Thus the believer, though never free from exposure to temptation, need not succumb to it. Indeed, spiritual believers are the more confronted with temptation.

It has been well said that spiritual believers are honored with warfare in the front line trenches. There the fiercest pressure of the enemy is felt. But they are also privileged to witness the enemy's crushing defeat; so abundant is the power of God, and thus highly is the spiritual believer honored.[1]

THE PURPOSES OF TEMPTATION

If temptation is universal there must be some reason for it— even possibly some good reason. And there is. For one thing, God uses testing to try and prove His children. Peter reminded some suffering saints of the first century: "Now for a season, if need be, ye are in heaviness through manifold temptations: that the trial of your faith, being much more precious than of gold that perisheth, though it be tried with fire, might be found unto praise and honour and glory at the appearing of Jesus Christ" (I Peter 1:6-7). In this passage the two principal words for temptation or testing are used. The one at the end of verse 6, translated "temptations," basically means to experience, pierce, attempt, and thus comes to indicate the concept of trying or testing. When this kind of testing or temptation originates from God, as it apparently did in the cases of Peter's readers, it cannot be a solicitation to evil but rather a testing in order to prove the Christian character of those so tempted. James clearly says that "God cannot be tempted with evil, neither tempteth He any man" (1:13). So when God tempts or tests, it is, as Peter says in verse 7, for the purpose of trying faith. That word usually includes the idea of a trial which is successfully passed and which consequently gives approval to the one tried. Paul earned such approval through the trials of the early years of his Christian life even before he began the first missionary journey. Having endured trials and testings, he was then able to say that he was approved of God who proved his heart (I Thess. 2:4). This kind of testing is not to bring out the worst in us, but the best.

Nevertheless, Satan can also be the source of temptation or testing (the first word, as used, e.g., in I Cor. 7:5), and his avowed purpose is to aim for our downfall. If we do yield to such a temptation, of course, we fail to find approval by God; rather we

1. Lewis Sperry Chafer, *He That Is Spiritual*, p. 182.

are disapproved. The second word, to prove, is never used in relation to Satan's tempting the Christian, since he obviously has no intention of giving the believer the opportunity to be approved.

I think the principal difficulty in sorting out the various ideas involved in this concept of temptation is that for most of us temptation means something evil in itself or at least something which leads to evil. It is inevitable that we have such an idea since men so often break down under temptation and are disapproved rather than approved. In other words, the English word *temptation* means to most only a solicitation to evil. We need also to remember that it has the idea of testing, trying, proving; and if God is the source there can be no solicitation to evil. Nevertheless, Satan and our own flesh may become involved, and these, not God, are the sources of evil. A circumstance of testing may be initiated by God to prove us; but at some point our flesh is enticed and draws us into an evil result (James 1:14-15). But God's purpose was to refine; Satan or our own sin natures may thwart that purpose.

Before concluding this discussion of the "testing" purpose of temptation as stated in I Peter 1:6-7, it is worth noting in the midst of such trials a believer may legitimately be in great sorrow and heaviness because of the test. He never loses his basic joy because of his secure spiritual condition (I Peter 1:3-6*a*), but that joy may be clouded over with the sorrow of the moment. It is an unrealistic concept of spirituality to think that joy and heaviness cannot go together. Indeed, it is unbiblical.

A second purpose for which God may bring testing into a believer's life is to teach him certain things he could not otherwise learn. That is why Peter exhorts us not to be surprised even at fiery trials since our Lord too suffered in the days of His flesh (I Peter 4:12-13). What did suffering do for the perfect God-Man? The Scripture says that He learned obedience through the things He suffered (Heb. 5:8). Thus testings and trials should teach believers obedience to God and His will.

Temptations may also be used to increase our love for God. "Blessed is the man that endureth temptation: for when he is tried, he shall receive the crown of life, which the Lord hath promised to them that love him" (James 1:12). Testings should also teach us patient endurance as it did for the early churches

(Rev. 2:3, 13). Testings also make us cast ourselves on God, learning dependence in ways we might not have known otherwise. These may come in the form of opposition to one's stand for Christ (II Cor. 1:8-10) or sometimes in the nature of physical affliction (II Cor. 12:7-9). These lessons which temptations can teach us—obedience, love, endurance, dependence—are necessary for complete maturity in the Christian life. Manifold temptations teach manifold lessons.

But as with all temptations, a test which God designed to teach us something may be failed and the lesson lost. In that case, the only solution is to confess the sin, pick oneself up again, learn the lesson of the weakness of the flesh, and lean harder on the power of God.

But, you say, are not the risks so great that God would do better to eliminate temptations from our lives? The answer is no, for testing is the route to approval and growth in our Christian lives. Proving requires testing; growth is faster in the face of opposition; great results involve great risks. Testings are God's way of offering us opportunities for approval and growth; they are the way of Satan's defeat. Which way we go depends largely on us.

Protection in Temptation

First Corinthians 10:13 is a great promise for all believers: "God is faithful, who will not suffer you to be tempted above that ye are able; but will with the temptation also make a way to escape, that ye may be able to bear it." Actually, God promises protection in temptation along two lines—the extent of it and the escape in it.

1. God guarantees to limit the intensity and kind of temptation to what He knows we can bear. This is an especially wonderful promise when you remember that it is based on His perfect and complete knowledge of our particular and individual capabilities to bear testing. It is not based on what we think we can bear, but what He knows we can. This means further that every test can not only be borne but successfully passed. No believer ever has the right to say that God expected too much of him in the light of this promise. How carefully God watched over the testings that came to Job; yet He was able to allow Satan to un-

leash his full fury against that man and his family because the
Lord knew that he could bear it. And he did. How often Paul
was pressed beyond measure yet never beyond bearing (II Cor.
1:8-10; 6:4-10). Even when he despaired of life itself, God was
measuring out the extent to which he could be tested. These illustrations indicate that large testing means large trust. God cannot allow the weak and immature believer to be tested severely
knowing he would not be able to bear it.

2. God promises to provide a way of escape—literally, the way
out. He makes this along with the temptation; and please notice,
He makes the test according to this verse. This reinforces what
we said in the preceding section about God needing to use testings in order to cause growth in our spiritual lives. The believer
who thinks he is living above temptation is living in a dream
world, not in the world God has designed for him. What is this
way out? It is clearly not escape from the experience; otherwise,
the last phrase in the verse would mean nothing, for a person
relieved of temptation does not bear it. Neither is it a promise
of deliverance from future tests; rather it is a promise of help
tailored for the particular trial to give strength to endure in the
midst of the temptation.

A similar promise is made in Hebrews 2:18: "For in that he
himself hath suffered being tempted, he is able to succour them
that are tempted." In the final analysis whatever way of escape
is provided in a particular situation, it will include dependence on
the sustaining power of the Lord. But it may also include the use
of other resources which God gives which we shall discuss in
the following section.

Notice, finally, in I Corinthians 10:13 that it is God who makes
the temptation and the way out—at the same time. These tests
that came into life are ordered by Him, and the way out in each
case is not an afterthought. Or, to put it another way, the moment the test begins, the way out is available. God does not wait
to see how we are going to make out in the test and then suddenly come up with a way out if we are yielding; the way out is there
all throughout the course of the test.

This is the promise of God which is our protection in every test
—a careful measuring out of the extent to which we may be tested,

and a consistent provision of an escape while we bear the experience.

Procedures to Use in Temptation

By example and direct teaching, the Bible gives a good deal of advice about how to meet temptation. The particulars fall into two categories: (1) general responsibilities in all circumstances, and (2) special resources for individual situations.

In the face of any and all temptation the believer has three general responsibilities. First, he is to rejoice in the midst of testing. "My brethren, count it all joy when ye fall into divers temptations" (James 1:2). This is not the attitude of a cynic or stoic but of a triumphant Christian who meets temptation not with passive resignation but with positive joy. This was the attitude of the early disciples who rejoiced that they were counted worthy to suffer shame for His name (Acts 5:41). Paul's testimony was that he rejoiced in tribulations (Rom. 5:3). How can this be? Paul and James answer in unison: We can rejoice because we know that a testing, successfully passed, will produce faith and patient endurance in the life, and sometimes this can only be done through tribulations.

Second, Christians have the responsibility to endure temptation. "Blessed is the man that endureth temptation" (James 1:12). We have already seen that the great promise of I Corinthians 10:13 does not promise relief from the temptation but help in enduring it. To endure means to bear the test with patience and constancy and without murmuring, fainting or blaspheming. One may ask, "Why did this happen?" But the believer who shows endurance will not question that God is working out His purpose in the test to produce growth and develop graces in his life. To yield is sin; to grumble is to fail; to endure is to learn the lesson God has designed through the test.

Third, the believer should be in prayer about temptation. One of the petitions of the Lord's Prayer is "Lead us not into temptation, but deliver us from evil [the evil one]" (Matt. 6:13). Knowing his weakness, the child of God should be asking his heavenly Father not to leave him to his own ways which would expose him to the overcoming power of the devil. This is a petition for those who realize that they are weak and susceptible to evil that

the Lord will not allow them to be too often or too sorely tried, and that, in the trials which may come, the devil will not gain the victory. This petition is not for heroes and idealists, but for ordinary folks who are realists about the weakness of the flesh and the possibilities for failure that are part of every test.

In addition to these general responsibilities there are some special resources listed in the Word to be used in times of temptation.

First and rather strangely, there are occasions when the believer will show the greatest strength and wisdom if he flees the situation involved in a temptation. Some overly pious people would consider this cowardly, but it is scriptural. The commands to do this are quite specific and clear. "Flee from idolatry" (I Cor. 10:14). "Flee also youthful lusts" (II Tim. 2:22). The examples are equally clear. On the first missionary journey Paul fled from Iconium when the opposition grew strong against him (Acts 14:5-6), and in this instance it was the better part of wisdom.

In Genesis 39 there is a beautiful example of the principle of fleeing. Joseph, a slave in Potiphar's house, was propositioned to commit adultery by Potiphar's wife. At the first solicitation he resolutely said no. He saw the consequences of yielding to this temptation in their proper light, for he said, "How can I do this great wickedness, and sin against God?" (v. 9). There was no dallying, no hesitation, no compromise. But temptation did not vanish with this first refusal, for Potiphar's wife solicited him "day by day" (v. 10). Finally "she caught him by his garment, saying, Lie with me: and he left his garment in her hand, and fled, and got him out" (v. 12). While the King James expression "got him out" is a bit quaint, it expresses the principle of fleeing temptation quite forcibly. Sometimes it *is* far better to flee a situation in which one might yield to the temptation than to stay and fight. This is no denial of the power of God but an honest appraisal of the weakness of the flesh.

A second resource which the believer has in some temptation situations is to destroy that which may become an instrument or means of sin. This principle is stated in Romans 13:14: "But put ye on the Lord Jesus Christ, and make not provision for the flesh,

to fulfil the lusts thereof." Not providing for the flesh may mean getting rid of certain things in the life which cause one to sin.

An excellent example of this is found in the events which occurred at Ephesus during Paul's ministry in that great city on his third missionary journey (Acts 19:11-20). As Christianity spread in the city, the new converts came under conviction about their possession and use of "curious arts" (v. 19). These were supposedly magical words and sayings written on scrolls and on amulets. Some were composed of letters which were written on the crown and girdle and feet of the statue of Diana which stood in the great temple of Diana at Ephesus. When the believers became convicted of their continued use of these "good luck" charms and books, they brought them together and burned the scrolls in a huge bonfire. The value of the scrolls alone was fifty thousand pieces of silver, which would be around fifteen thousand dollars, according to one computation. Although it is impossible to determine the exact value of these materials, they were certainly very costly.

Today, of course, we would be much too wise and advanced to have a book burning. Even if we thought that such things as rabbits' feet, four-leaf clovers, astrology packets and the daily horoscope in the newspaper were out of place in a Christian's life, we would not be so unwise as to lose the monetary value of these items by destroying them. We would probably appoint a committee to head a drive to collect all these things and sell them to the used book dealers. Then, naturally, the money received could go into the building fund! But, of course, what would happen is that affluent Christians of our day would shortly find their way to the bookstores and buy back the donated books. Perhaps that's a clever way to raise money, but it definitely is no way to overcome temptation. Sometimes outright destruction of those things which entice us to sin is the only way to spiritual victory.

Recently I was speaking at a young people's camp on this subject using the incident in Acts 19 as an illustration. Although I had mentioned no applications of this to modern life, the Holy Spirit spoke to a fellow in the audience who had come to know Christ only a few weeks before about the kind of music which was a very big part of his life. The result was that he literally destroyed songs and records which he owned and which he realized

stirred up passions in his heart and mind. Notes on a music staff and words are not in themselves sinful, but they can be put together in a way that entices and stirs up desires which can lead to sin. If so, the best course of action may be to get rid of them.

Other illustrations would not be difficult to cite. Usually the "thing" involved is not in or of itself wrong, but it may become a tool to defeat us. Realizing our weaknesses, it is best not to have around that which provides opportunity for the flesh to fulfill its lusts. This is a way to victory.

A third resource which the believer may use to help him overcome temptation is good company. After advising Timothy to flee youthful lusts, Paul adds: "But follow righteousness, faith, charity [love], peace, with them that call on the Lord out of a pure heart" (II Tim. 2:22). Good companions can help prevent temptation taking the wrong course. The proverb puts it this way: "He who walks with wise men becomes wise, but the companion of fools will suffer harm" (13:20, RSV). Associating with the enemies of Christ was one of the steps that led to Peter's denial the night before the crucifixion (Luke 22:55).

This is not to say that we can never associate with unsaved friends lest they lead us into temptation, but it is to say that when any companionship, Christian or unbelieving, tends to draw us down to any low level, we must shun it like poison, for that's what it is.

This is what the Bible has to say about temptation. God designs to use it to prove, teach and increase our love for Him. No solicitation to evil ever comes from Him. That happens when we are drawn away of our own lusts and enticed (James 1:14). But God has promised never to put upon us more than we can bear successfully and to give us help and resources in the bearing. The spiritual Christian can expect to be tempted; and the spiritual Christian will pass through temptation with flying colors!

14

CONFESSING AND FORGIVING

An area of the spiritual life which has raised a number of practical questions today is that related to the confession of sin. What is confession? When should it be made? Should it be public and/or private? Hasn't God forgiven us already whether we confess or not? What is our obligation in regard to forgiving one another? These are some of the questions to which various answers are being given, and they are questions that must be answered, but from the Scriptures.

Confessing Our Sins

1. What is confession? The word *confess* means, literally, to say the same thing; that is, to agree or to acknowledge fully. Thus a confession is an acknowledgment of agreement with a standard and includes an admission of a previous disagreement. When one confesses Christ as Saviour, he acknowledges that what he previously thought of Christ was wrong and that now he agrees with God that the death of Christ paid for his sins. When a Christian confesses specific sins in his life, he agrees with what God says about that sin and acknowledges his past disagreement or guilt. The standard is always God's Word uncompromised.

2. Will confession always include repentance and turning from sin? This is not an easy question to answer. One would like to say, yes, true confession will always involve turning from that sin which has been confessed. Undoubtedly this is the way it ought to be, but it is not always so. What saint hasn't fallen back into the very sin he had previously confessed and (he thought) forsaken?

What is the answer? On the one hand it is quite clear just from the meaning of the word that confession is no mere mouthing of

144

a particular sin. Agreeing with God about a sin includes not only acknowledging that He says it is sin, but also having His viewpoint on sin which would certainly include forsaking it. Not to include the attitude of expecting to turn from that sin would be only partial agreement with God concerning the matter. Thus true confession cannot be a mere putting of words into something that automatically grinds out forgiveness.

On the other hand, why is it that so many have the experience of confessing, turning away from that sin, and yet falling back into it again? The fault apparently does not lie in a confession which was defective but rather in not appropriating the means available to give victory over the problem. And yet sometimes that is not the whole story either, for there are some who, in spite of all that can be done, lapse into the same sin again, overwhelmed by the power of the flesh or of Satan. But the confession was not deficient in such instances. You see, we need to distinguish between several things: the confession, the subsequent life, the power of sin. In other words, there seems to be no guarantee in the Word that even when sin is confessed and forsaken the believer will be exempt from ever falling into it for the rest of his life. Thus true confession must include sorrow for sin and a turning from it, but true confession does not guarantee even that particular sin will never be committed again. If it is, then it must be confessed again.

3. When must we confess our sins? In general the answer is Whenever sin comes to our attention and we are ready and willing to acknowledge it as sin and turn from it. But in particular the Scripture places two time limits on this matter. The first is nighttime and the second is Communion time. The principle of Ephesians 4:26—"Let not the sun go down upon your wrath"—seems to indicate that the slate should be cleared before retiring at night. The day's activities, including its mistakes, can conveniently be reviewed then and confession to the Lord made. But if this is not done the night's sleep and next day's activities may bring with them an insensitivity and forgetfulness which in turn may lead to greater sin, or at least to continued loss of fellowship because of the unconfessed sin.

Communion time, when the Lord's Supper is taken, is also a time for self-examination and confession of sin. Not to do so may

bring judgment from God in the form of sickness or even physical death (I Cor. 11:27-32). Ideally, sin should be confessed when it comes to light, but it should not go unconfessed beyond bedtime; if for some reason it does, never beyond Communion time.

4. Is there more than one way to confess? So far in the discussion we have been implying that confession is a recital to God, either verbally or silently, of our sins in prayer. Certainly this is one way to confess. But a confession may also be made in the form of a thought which even in a moment of time encompasses recital, acknowledgment, forsaking and all that is involved in a true confession. Too, a confession may take the form of a resolution to change one's ways. Indeed, all confession should result in this, but this may be the only form a particular confession takes. That sort of confession speaks very loudly.

I experienced one time a rather lengthy meeting in which confessions were being made publicly by students in a school. A number of these were quite necessary and had a beneficial effect. But there was one girl in particular whose confession did not quite ring true. It was long enough and detailed, though really not specific, but it seemed to be sugar-coated with an artificial piety. In due time the routine of school life closed in once again, and life was being lived again in the valley. One day not long after, I found myself standing in the cafeteria line for lunch when this particular girl cut in at the head of the line. A student standing in front of me turned to another one and said, "I see she's up to her old tricks. It's too bad she didn't get the victory over cutting into the line!" Sometimes it's better to see than to hear a confession.

5. What about public confession? We want to deal with this later in more detail, but suffice it to say now that primarily confession is to God. Nevertheless, there are occasions when some sort of public acknowledgment of sin is necessary and appropriate. The public may simply be one other person (Matt. 5:21) or the entire church (Matt. 18:17), and with such confession there may or may not be the need for restitution.

It is important to remember that public confession of specific sins is often completely inappropriate. A changed life is a public confession, but the enumerating of certain sins in public may be entirely out of place. I was personally troubled about this at one

point in my life, and I asked a very wise and elderly saint what he would advise as guidelines in relation to the public confession of sin. He offered two: (1) Whose voice is prompting the public confession—God's, Satan's or your own? Unless it is God who definitely leads to do this, it should not be done. Too often we can talk ourselves into the apparent advisability of making a public confession. (2) Will this public confession edify the church or not? The Bible is quite clear that all things in the public meetings of the church are to be done unto edification and in a decent and orderly manner (I Cor. 14:26, 40). Any public confession that would violate these guidelines is better left unspoken.

6. What kind of forgiveness results from confession? Since the Christian life is a family relationship, the matter of forgiveness can be best viewed in that context. We enter the family when we acknowledge Jesus Christ as our personal Saviour. That new birth into the family of God is eternal; we will never be cut off from the family. Nevertheless, relationships within the family are similar to those in an earthly family. Sometimes there comes a break in fellowship between the father and his child. Disobedience to the father's will does this, and while it does not expel the child from the family, it does affect his fellowship and the enjoyment of his relationships and privileges in the family life. The same thing happens when we sin against our heavenly Father. He does not cast us out but He is grieved and we cannot enjoy full fellowship in the family. The blood of Christ once shed is effective to keep us in the family even when we sin (I John 1:7), and the advocate (or patron or attorney or friend) we have in the Lord Jesus constantly takes our case when we sin and reminds the Father that His death paid for all our sins (I John 2:1).

The eternal fellowship of belonging to the family can never be broken, but temporal fellowship of enjoying the family can be interrupted by sin. The blood of Christ maintains eternal fellowship; our confession regains the lost fellowship of the moment. When we confess "he is faithful and just to forgive us our sins, and to cleanse us from all unrighteousness" (I John 1:9).

But family-of-God relationships are not only with the Father but they also involve other members of the family, other Christians. To maintain proper fellowship with other believers the Bible emphasizes the need for a forgiving spirit.

Forgiving One Another

Confessing our sins is necessary for fellowship in God's family and so is forgiving one another. Indeed, there is a very clear principle in the New Testament, and it is this: Family fellowship with God depends on family fellowship with one another. Or, to put it another way, good relations with the Father depend on good relations with His children.

1. The principle in precept (Matt. 5:21-26). In this interesting part of the Sermon on the Mount the Lord declares that little things harbored often lead to terrible sin. A little thing like anger against a brother may very well lead to murder and thus to hell (vv. 21-22). Likewise, a little thing like a brother having something against you leads to loss of fellowship with your heavenly Father (vv. 23-24). Indeed, so important is it to have things right between members of the family of God that this takes precedence over bringing a gift to God. Notice how far-reaching this precept is, for it is not a matter of the sinning brother admitting his wrong before there can be a reconciliation. If you (apparently innocent in the matter) remember that someone else has something against you (even unjustly so), it is your responsibility to go to him and seek a reconciliation. Most of us operate on the principle that the person in the wrong should take the first step, and if he doesn't then we have no obligation to right the situation. Not so, said the Lord. You must show the forgiving spirit by going to him and trying to make things right. Otherwise, your service and worship of God will be affected adversely. Good relations with the Father depend on good relations with His children.

2. The principle in parable (Matt. 18:21-35). But suppose a brother keeps on sinning against me? Am I obliged to keep on forgiving him? In the time of Christ the rabbis said that one was required to forgive the same person only three times. When Peter approached the Lord on this point he thought by suggesting seven times that he was showing a great magnanimous spirit (v. 21). But the Lord said that forgiveness of one another should be unlimited, because that is the kind of forgiveness God gives us. Then he recited a parable about the servant who owed his lord an impossible debt (perhaps about $10 million by today's values) and who when he pleaded with that lord was forgiven the entire

amount. But then the forgiven man turned right around and demanded payment of a twenty-five-dollar debt from a fellow servant. The Lord makes two points from this parable: the forgiving Father ought to be imitated by His children (vv. 32-33), and an unforgiving person cannot expect to be forgiven himself (v. 35).

3. The principle in picture (John 13:1-17). When the Lord washed the feet of His disciples He gave a vivid illustration of forgiveness. Actually, there are two facets to the illustration. His washing of the disciples' feet pictures His keeping us clean by His constant ministry of intercession. We have been washed at salvation, but we need to be kept in fellowship, which He does for us by washing our feet (v. 10). This is the same ministry as mentioned in I John 2:2.

But the Lord also gave a command on the basis of this illustration: "Ye also ought to wash one another's feet" (v. 14). This can only mean that we ought to forgive one another just as He forgives us. Unfortunately, many read this passage and see only Christ's work for the believer and not the believer's work for one another. And it is the ministry of forgiving one another. Notice again that the innocent party takes the initiative in forgiving the one whose feet are dirty.

There are some interesting details about washing one another's feet that are suggested by the Lord's action that night before His crucifixion. For one thing, He made no grand announcement about what He was going to do. Foot washing should be done silently. Obviously, too, one who washes another's feet has to get down to where the feet are! You cannot lord it over another believer if you are in the position of washing his feet. And this is exactly what we are exhorted to remember in Galatians 6:1: "Brethren, if a man be overtaken in a fault, ye which are spiritual, restore such an one in the spirit of meekness; considering thyself, lest thou also be tempted." The spiritual Christian takes the initiative to restore the sinning brother; but he must do it meekly, remembering always that he too might have been caught in the same sin. The imagery also suggests that the forgiveness must be complete. This can be no halfhearted act, for only partially washing dirty feet results in muddy feet, not clean ones. One cannot have the attitude "I forgive you, but. . . ."

4. The principle in prayer (Matt. 6:12). In the model prayer the Lord reminded His disciples (and us) that only if we forgive others can we expect our Father to forgive us (not in salvation, but in the life and relationships of the family). The petition which indicates that in the prayer should be translated "Forgive us our debts as we have forgiven our debtors." In other words, good relations with the Father depend on good relations with His children. It is instructive to notice that of all the things in the Lord's Prayer which might have been singled out for attention, only this matter is (vv. 14-15). It is obviously of primary importance.

5. The principle in practice. It is not easy to practice this principle of forgiveness, so may I offer several suggestions which may help.

First, as we have seen over and over, I must not wait to forgive until my brother sees and admits his wrong. As soon as I see it I am to forgive whether or not he ever sees it. This may mean that I go to him and seek to show him the error (as Gal. 6:1 indicates), or I may not be in a position to speak with him personally. But in either case I must forgive.

Second, this principle, like most others, should first be practiced on those closest to us. Most of us do not have any problem forgiving people unknown to us or those whose sin little affects us. This is a matter primarily of forgiving fellow church members rather than those of another denomination. It concerns my fellow students, my pastor and my fellow Sunday school teachers.

Third, in practicing forgiveness I do not condone sin. One can forgive and still disagree in areas where there might be a genuine difference of opinion. This principle does not operate to override our convictions, but it should work to keep our feelings and attitudes right with each other and with the Lord. I would want to be the last ever to say that scriptural convictions should be compromised; but I want to be the first to say that forgiving one another is a scriptural command and absolutely essential to the maintenance of a healthy spiritual life.

Confessing our sins and forgiving one another—these are constant needs in the spiritual life. Confessing keeps us right with God and other believers; forgiving keeps us right with other believers and with God.

15

LEGAL OR LEGALISTIC?

THE COMPLEXITIES of the Christian life are multiplying every year. It used to be fairly simple to determine what was right or wrong for a believer even in the area of debatable things; but today not only are more things debated but there seems to be more disagreement even among Christian leaders about these matters. Many of us grew up in days (not so long ago, either!) when there were no television, no full-length Walt Disney movies, and no Sunday pro football. Just the existence of some of these new attractions has intensified the complications. Add to this the feeling of many Christians that the whole concept of law and legalism in the Christian life must be rethought, and you have a picture that is increasingly complex. But the Bible must have answers and guidelines to these problems which will work even in this sophisticated twentieth century.

At the very outset, let's clarify some things about law and grace. For one thing, they are antithetical concepts, and that antithesis is vitally related to the Christian life. When Paul answers the question of why sin shall not have dominion over the believer, it is with the statement that we are not under law but under grace (Rom. 6:14). Here, in relation to our sanctification, being "under grace" is set in sharp contrast to being "under law." In other words, law and grace in this context seem to be opposites, and the only way for a Christian to experience a holy life is by being under grace.

In what sense are they opposites? In the sense of a rule of life under which people live, law was one and grace is another. That is, just prior to Christ's coming, people were expected to live according to the rule of life detailed in the Mosaic law; today the code under which God's people live is called grace because it is

151

the law of Christ who brought grace to this world (John 1:17). Now a rule of life involves at least three aspects: the specific laws, the enabling power and the motivation. Thus when we speak of law and grace as rules of life we include not only the specific commands but also the power and motivation which are part of the rule of life. And in this sense law and grace are antithetical opposites, for the laws, the power and the motivation were different under law from what they are under grace. Specifically it looks like this:

	Law	*Grace*
Laws	613 commandments in the law of Moses	Hundreds of equally specific commands in the law of Christ
Power	Holy Spirit (but not permanently guaranteed)	Indwelling Spirit (permanently guaranteed)
Motivation	Primarily "have to" and fear	Primarily "want to" and love

Though somewhat oversimplified, this shows the antithesis between law and grace when conceived of as rules of life for God's people.

But in another sense, law and grace are not sharply antithetical, for there was grace under law and there is law under grace. This is a very important point for holy living which is often misunderstood by believers. There are those, for instance, who so sharply contrast law and grace that they conclude that there can be no specific laws under today's grace standard. To introduce any laws becomes to them legalism. Unfortunately, too, this doctrinal confusion sometimes becomes the basis for a loose kind of living which is justified in the name of practicing Christian liberty.

The truth of the matter is that there was grace under the Mosaic law (a truth we cannot develop here) and there is law under grace. The New Testament speaks of the "perfect law of liberty" (James 1:25), the "royal law" (James 2:8), the law of Christ" (Gal. 6:2) and the "law of the Spirit of life" (Rom. 8:2). It is, of course, the specific commands of the New Testament

which compose the law of Christ, and it is not difficult to remember that there are hundreds of such commands. They cover every area of life and they are so definite that they may be termed a law. And they are a vital part of what it means to be "under grace."

To try to understand this further, let's examine some of the categories of life under grace and characteristics of those who are living this life.

SOME THINGS ARE LEGAL

It is always right or legal to do certain things under grace. These are the clear, positive commands of the New Testament which the believer is expected to follow. He need not debate them, nor question them, nor seek underlying principles in them, nor pray about whether or not he should obey them. They are definite, clear and obligatory.

The list could be very long, but here are some examples. It is always legal for every soul to be subject to government (Rom. 13:1); it is always right to do everything in the church decently and in order (I Cor. 14:40); we should bear one another's burdens (Gal. 6:2); wives should submit to their husbands (Eph. 5:22); the thoughts of the mind should be controlled (Phil. 4:8) as should one's speech (Col. 4:6); we are to pray without ceasing (I Thess. 5:17). Good deeds are always legal (II Thess. 3: 13); sober-minded thinking is always appropriate (Titus 2:2, 4, 6); and the example of the life of Christ is the pattern for the believer's conduct (I Peter 2:21; I John 2:6). In other words, all the positive aids to sanctification are always legal for the believer.

SOME THINGS ARE ILLEGAL

Though some do not like to admit it, it is true that there are negatives in Christianity. Some things are always wrong for the believer. It is illegal to be conformed to this world (Rom. 12:2), to be an idolator (I Cor. 10:7), to grieve the Holy Spirit (Eph. 4: 30), to provoke one's children to wrath (Col. 3:21), to quench the Spirit (I Thess. 5:19), to be ashamed of the testimony of the Lord (II Tim. 1:8), to forsake the assembling of ourselves together (Heb. 10:25), to speak evil of one another (James 4:11), to render evil for evil (I Peter 3:9), to receive a teacher of false

doctrine into one's house (II John 10). These, plus many other specific negatives, are never right for the spiritual Christian.

SOME THINGS ARE LEGAL AND ILLEGAL

There is no problem at least in understanding matters that are clearly right or wrong for the believer. While there may be a problem in being willing to obey them, at least the precepts are clear. However, many things the Christian faces are under some circumstances right and under others wrong. This is because the thing itself (and many complex aspects of life are included in this category) is not right or wrong—it is without morality; or sometimes it is because a right thing may become wrong under certain circumstances or within certain relationships. For instance, cloth is amoral, but the way it is used may result in modest or immodest apparel (I Tim. 2:9). Food is a proper and necessary thing, but excessive use of it will result in intemperance and gluttony which are sin.

There are many aspects of life in which a course of action is not always easy to determine. Let me raise a few questions without any prejudice as to how they should be answered in order to illustrate the complexity of issues facing an earnest Christian today. Football and baseball are healthy activities both for participation and observation. This is clear. But does the picture change when these sports occur on Sunday? Should a believer attend a professional game on the Lord's Day? What about watching them on television on Sunday? Should his children be forbidden or permitted to play in the backyard on Sunday? These are legitimate questions about something which in itself is good but which may become debatable by being related to the Lord's Day.

Similar problems can be raised with a seemingly uncomplicated commodity like film. Whether its use is religious or secular is not a criterion by which its propriety or impropriety can be judged, for many Christians use it to take secular scenes and purely for pleasure. Where the film may be shown is no longer a criterion either, for very bad films can now be seen at home on television, and fine religious ones can be viewed in theaters. And the complications are growing with the increased use of this art form for Christian education purposes.

Or take investing in stocks. I have an acquaintance who, on conviction, will never invest in tobacco or liquor stocks, and in my judgment this is highly commendable. One day I asked him if he owned stock in a certain chemical company, which he did. Then I inquired if he knew that that particular company was one of the largest manufacturers of the paper used in making cigarettes. This he did not know, but he concluded that the diversity of that company's operations and products would permit him to continue to hold its stock. Or what if you discovered that a large part of the profits of a chain of food stores went to the support of a major cult in this country? Would you feel free to hold that stock? Or should you contribute to the profits by even buying their products at the store?

Sometimes the argument is advanced that Christians should avoid having anything to do with certain industries because the people engaged in them seem to be more wicked than the general run of the populace. Perhaps this is so, but where do you draw the line? It could well be that your milkman is a very wicked person, or who knows what kind of person cut the lumber for the chair you are sitting on? There are wicked people in every occupation; to avoid them completely would be impossible.

Or again, the atmosphere of certain places is supposed to put them off limits to believers, and in many instances this is a valid principle. But the cursing and drinking one often sees and hears at sports events doesn't exactly create the best atmosphere for your wife or children to be exposed to. Where do you draw the line?

How does an earnest believer decide these complex problems? Although the Bible does not give direct answers to many specific problems, it does lay down guiding principles which can be applied to such situations. Here are some of them.

1. Use but do not abuse the world. Paul makes it quite clear that the Christian has to live in the world and use the things of it, including associations with undesirable people. The only alternative to this is to leave the world (I Cor. 5:10). This is what I would call separation by suicide! Since this is not recommended, one must use the world and the things and people in it. But Paul also warns us not to abuse even good things (I Cor. 7:31). Notice some of the things he mentions in the context of this passage:

sorrow, joy, buying and selling, care of one's wife. All these things are good and legal, but they may become illegal for the believer because of abuse of them. And then they are wrong. Where is that fine line between proper use and sinful abuse? That is not always easy to determine, but the Lord can and will show any of His children who ask Him about it.

2. Enjoy but do not love the world. The spiritual believer has a perfect biblical right to enjoy the things that God gives him (I Tim. 6:17). A very sacrificial person may be quite carnal because he may be quite proud of his sacrifices; whereas spirituality can be exhibited in abundance and plenty. Believers need not apologize if God gives them something; actually there is nothing quite so fraudulently pious than to hear a Christian excusing what he has. "I got such a bargain" is often used to justify having things. Now, I am the first with my Scotch background to look for a bargain, but we need to remember that if having a certain thing is wrong in the first place, getting it at a discount does not necessarily make it right! If God gives it to you, do not apologize for it, and feel free to enjoy it.

On the other hand we are commanded not to love the world or the things in it (I John 2:15). This seems to mean Don't make an idol of anything that even God may give you; rather find your sufficiency in Him so that if all the things you have were taken away you would still be a happy Christian. It is not easy to strike a balance between proper enjoying and improper loving. Some people never enjoy what God allows them to have because they are afraid they might love and idolize these things too much; others enjoy so much that they do idolize. It is the spiritual believer who will learn how to handle these things that are legal and keep them that way.

3. Never hinder the spiritual growth of another Christian. In this realm of activities, particularly, what you may feel free to do may be a genuine hindrance to another believer's growth. If so, then the Bible rightly says not to do it (I Cor. 8:13). To do it would, under such circumstances, be sin. In other words, a legal activity becomes illegal if another believer is hindered.

But how is one to know if something is a genuine hindrance or whether the person who objects to your doing something is simply trying to impose his Christian standard on you? This is not an

easy question to answer. On the one hand, it is true that if you look long and far enough you can probably find some other Christian who will object to just about anything you may want to do. On the other hand, one must be careful not to become insensitive to the feelings and consciences of other believers, for to do so is to sin against them. How does one strike the balance?

There are two guidelines that have helped me personally. The first is this: Is the objecting person really trying to grow and make progress in his own spiritual life, or is he simply sitting on the sidelines of the racecourse sniping at the runners? If he is actually running with me in the race, then I want to do everything possible to help him to be a winner too. But if he is simply a self-appointed judge of all the runners while he himself is making little or no progress in the Christian life, I do not feel obliged to cater to his feelings or conscience.

The second is this: How many are apparently affected by what I may feel free to do? This was one of the guidelines used by the early church to ask the Gentile believers to curb their liberty in Christ, for there were simply too many Jewish Christians whose spiritual lives were being stunted by the legitimate practices of the Gentile converts (Acts 15:19-29). This principle can guide us when moving from one section of the country to another where believers have different standards or when crossing cultural or national boundaries.

Thus the two guidelines are: Who is hindered—a runner or a laggard? And how many are affected? But the overall principle is Do not do anything that will hinder the growth of another believer. Or, stated positively, do everything possible, including restricting your freedom, to encourage the spiritual life of your fellow believer.

4. Do all to the glory of God (I Cor. 10:31). This, of course, is the great summary guiding principle for the Christian life. The question Does this thing or practice conform to God's glory? can and should be asked by the spiritual believer of all aspects of his life. What is the glory of God? It is the manifestation of any or all of His attributes. In other words, it is the displaying of God to the world. Thus, things which glorify God are things which show the characteristics of His being to the world.

The principles are clear; sometimes the application of them is

difficult. But no believer should compound the difficulty because he is unwilling to obey God's Word.

SOME THINGS ARE LEGISLATED

It is quite proper in the Christian life for some believers to legislate rules of conduct for others. I am sure that a statement like that brings immediate and varied reaction—much of it negative—but it is nonetheless true. Some things are properly legislated in Christian conduct. This is not a violation of grace, for we saw at the beginning of this chapter that there are laws under what we label as the age of grace. Neither is legislation legalism as we shall see in the following section. It is sometimes scriptural to legislate.

There are two areas in which this is especially true, the area of conduct in the home and proper conduct in the church. The command to children to obey their parents certainly includes specific commands which are not mentioned in the Bible but which, nevertheless, are necessary, legitimate and binding on the children. For instance, the Bible says nothing about how late a young person should be allowed to stay out at night; yet the control of this is a very proper area for parents to regulate, and it is one which affects the Christian testimony of both parents and the young person in that family.

Twice in Hebrews 13 we are reminded that there are rulers in the local church (vv. 7, 17) who in the exercise of their responsibilities will have to set guidelines, exercise authority and discipline, and make rules for the members. Exactly what this may involve or how far it may go is not stated, but the principle is clearly established. Without it, there would be anarchy in the church.

Presumably the same principle would apply to other Christian organizations such as schools and mission boards. If a believer is a member of these groups, he is expected to give obedience and allegiance to them; if he cannot, then he will have to dissociate himself. Actually, when there is disagreement between those ruled and those ruling there are only three alternatives: obey anyway, try to change the rules if procedures are allowed for this, or sever connections.

SOME PEOPLE ARE LEGALISTIC

Legalism is more often talked about than defined, and when it is defined it is sometimes done to justify the practice of the one defining it and condemn the conduct of others! Of course, it must be realized that legalism is not a biblical word, so any definition is derived from implications of the Scripture, not direct statements. Perhaps the simplest way to understand legalism is to define what it is not and by process of elimination see what it is.

It is of primary importance to understand that legalism is not the presence of laws. This is, unfortunately, what most people understand it to be, and the moment any law appears on their horizon they cry "Legalism!" If the presence of law is legalism, then, of course, God would have to be charged with promoting it since He has given man innumerable laws during human history. Further, parents and church leaders and governmental authorities would also be legalists, if that be a proper concept of legalism. Legalism is not the presence of laws.

Furthermore, some define legalism as the imposition of law on someone else. But again such a definition fails to include the biblical sanction for parents and church leaders imposing laws upon their family and church group. Neither the presence of law nor the imposition of law is the key to understanding legalism.

What is legalism? It is a wrong attitude toward the code of laws under which a person lives. Legalism involves the presence of law, the wrong motive toward obeying that law and often the wrong use of the power provided to keep the law, but it is basically a wrong attitude. Thus legalism may be defined as "a fleshly attitude which conforms to a code for the purpose of exalting self." The code is whatever objective standard is applicable to man at a particular time (today it is the law of Christ); the motive is to exalt self and gain merit rather than to glorify God because of what He has done; and the power used to obey the code is that of the flesh, not that of the Holy Spirit. It is very important to note that a legalist *keeps* the law; he is not a violator of the law. Not to obey the law of Christ is lawlessness, not liberty. To obey it to exalt self is legalism. The legalist and the nonlegalist will both give at least outward conformity to the law under which they are living.

Let's test this concept. Look, first, at a man living under the Mosaic law. All Israelites who lived under the law had to do certain things in order to maintain their proper relationship to the commonwealth of Israel. The legalist obeyed to exalt himself, and this is the type of conduct which Isaiah so severely condemned (1:11-15). On the other hand, the Israelite who was led and motivated by God to bring his sacrifices and offerings in order to glorify God exhibited the right attitude. But both men brought sacrifices and obeyed the law under which they lived.

It cannot be emphasized too strongly that *having* to do something is *not* legalism, but the wrong attitude toward doing it is. In the example above both Israelites had to bring sacrifices; otherwise they would have suffered certain penalties. Their attitude toward what they had to do determined their legalism or absence of it. Or to use a nonbiblical illustration, a serious athlete has to keep training rules. Most athletes are glad to keep them, rigid as they may be, for the sheer love of sports. A few conform in order to make the team and glorify or show off themselves. The right attitude is love of sports; the wrong show-off attitude is legalism. But both attitudes relate to the same code of rules, and both produce conformity.

Under grace we have to do certain things. We are expected to keep the positive commands; we are obliged not to violate the negative ones; we must exercise spiritual sense in applying the principles of the Bible in debatable areas; and we are required to follow the rules legislated in the family and church groups. If one gives obedience in order to glorify God he is not a legalist. Even if one doesn't want to obey or doesn't understand why church leaders, for instance, set down certain rules, but nevertheless obeys in order to glorify God, this is not legalism. On the other hand, refusal to conform can be legalism because a nonconformist (even though he may have a perfect right to be one) is often glorifying self by parading his "liberty" to all the world. And that parading has made him a legalist.

So some Christians are legalists, not because law is legalism, but because a wrong attitude, which any of us can have, is. Right living is letting the glory of God motivate every action and letting the Spirit of God empower them, including those things which we have to do in order to conform to the law of Christ.

Some People Are Liberated

The precise opposite of liberty is slavery, not legalism (though of course legalistic living does involve a kind of slavery). The biblical concept of Christian liberty is the new position in Christ of freedom from the bondage and slavery of sin and the flesh (Rom. 6:22; II Peter 2:19). A believer may be in the position of liberty but practice legalism in the conduct of his life. Position and attitude are not the same; therefore, liberty and legalism are not exact opposites.

To be sure, the position of liberty which every Christian has does have a correspondingly correct practice. Liberty has brought us the freedom to be a slave of righteousness (Rom. 6:18). Note very carefully that Christian liberty does not give the believer the option of living any way he pleases; it is not license. It places him in a position where he can live as God pleases, something he was unable to do as an unregenerated person. Liberated living is not unrestricted living.

What, then, are the biblical limitations of a liberated Christian life? The answer to this question is extremely important in relation to sanctification, for unrestricted liberty is license, and wrongly restricted liberty is legalism. Biblically restricted liberty is liberated spiritual living. What is the right restriction? The answer is love. Paul put it succinctly: "For, brethren, ye have been called unto liberty; only use not liberty for an occasion to the flesh, but by love serve one another" (Gal. 5:13).

What is love? Usually we begin to think of it as an emotional expression in kind acts. That is a good description as far as it goes. But love is sometimes expressed in acts of correction because it wants to produce good or prevent wrong; and this, too, is love. The mother who cuddles her child also slaps its hand, and both are expressions of love. What is good? The believer realizes that ultimately good must be defined in terms of the will of God. Thus love is seeking the will of God in the one loved, and Christian liberty is to be restricted by that kind of love.

Such love-limited liberty will show itself in a spiritual Christian's actions. This is what is behind the principle of I Corinthians 8: 13. Certainly, Paul says, a Christian has the right to eat meat offered to idols, but some believers do not feel free to exercise

that right. Therefore, those who feel they can eat, should restrict their liberty out of love for the other brother. Note carefully that *both* the stronger and weaker brother refrain from eating though for different reasons.

Love-limited liberty will also manifest itself in the believer's attitude. Too often a Christian will curb his actions and still have a bad attitude toward the weaker brother. Likewise, the weaker brother can exhibit a wrong attitude by judging the stronger brother even for feeling free to do something whether he does it or not (Rom. 14:3). Both are wrong with such attitudes.

Liberated living is love-limited living, and this is true spirituality. We have said before that one of the primary evidences of spirituality is Christlikeness. And He who had freedom, limited only by the nature of God Himself, voluntarily took upon Himself the restrictions of the form of a servant in order that He might serve us. His liberty was limited by His great love for us, and our liberated position in Christ ought to be exhibited daily in a life of service. Only then do we follow the example of our Lord. "We then that are strong ought to bear the infirmities of the weak, and not to please ourselves. Let every one of us please his neighbour for his good to edification. For even Christ pleased not himself" (Rom. 15:1-3*a*).

16

SHOULD I SEEK TO SPEAK
IN TONGUES?

THERE IS NO DOUBT about the fact that the Bible teaches that tongues is a genuine spiritual gift. Neither is there any doubt that not a few Christians claim to have that gift and to experience results from it that seem beneficial to their spiritual lives. With the spread of tongues to groups outside those commonly associated with it, many believers are wondering if this is something they should seek in order to enhance their spiritual growth. Have I really experienced everything God wants me to have if I do not seek the gift of tongues?

Of course, the answer to this and all questions about tongues must be found in what the Bible says about the matter, not what somebody's experience seems to prove or disprove. This is not to say that the experiences which many are having today are not real; of course, they are. However, the all-important question is Are they scriptural experiences? You see, it is quite possible to have a genuine experience which, even though not against the Scripture, is not a biblical one. The only way to determine if any experience is biblical is to test the experience by the Bible and never vice versa.

Years ago I was helping in a church work in which there was a lady who was always dreaming dreams about me and the two other "young preachers" in the work. Through dreams she would communciate messages from God to us, and the messages always contained kind thoughts, comforting words and scriptural sentiments. Never, to my recollection, was there anything unscriptural in them; yet it was open to serious question whether this dear Christian lady was having a genuine biblical experience in

163

communicating revelation from God through her dreams. Experience must always be tested by the Bible as our final authority.

What can we learn about tongues from the Bible which will help us to know what place this gift may play in a balanced spiritual life? If we approach this matter positively (note the way the question was phrased—"What can we learn . . . ?"), perhaps we will be able to avoid much of the fruitless discussion which often accompanies this subject. Here are five things we can know definitely.

1. You can be baptized by the Spirit and not speak in tongues. As we have seen, every Christian has been baptized by the Spirit and thus placed in the body of Christ. This is an experience which occurs only once for each believer. In contrast, the filling of the Spirit may be experienced repeatedly and brings power in the Christian's life as he yields control. But the presence of tongues is not a necessary accompaniment or proof of the baptism of the Spirit. Notice the case of the Corinthians. Paul said (I Cor. 14:5) that all of them did not speak in tongues, and yet he made it plain that they all had been baptized with the Spirit (I Cor. 12:13). Obviously, then, some had been baptized who had not spoken in tongues. Furthermore, not once in either letter to that church did Paul exhort those who had not spoken in tongues to seek to do so. It is not a necessary sign of the baptism with the Spirit, and any teaching which insists on this is not following the Scripture.

2. The distribution of spiritual gifts is limited in various ways. For one, not every Christian has all the gifts. Indeed, it is doubtful if any believer (with the possible exception of some of the apostles) is given all the gifts. It is this variety in combination of gifts that each of us possesses that makes us dependent on each other for the proper functioning of the body of Christ.

Furthermore, not all the gifts are necessarily given to each generation of Christians, although we are often told that if God gave a certain gift in one generation He must give it in every generation because He is the same. This reasoning is frequently used to promote the more spectacular gifts today, but there are two fallacies behind this kind of thinking. First of all, God's "sameness" of power is not affected by a change in His program. Giving a gift to one generation and withholding it from the next does not

mean God's power is in any way lessened; it only indicates a change in His program. Or to change the example—if God decided to send an earthquake to release Paul and Silas from a Philippian jail and later decided not to release Paul from his Roman death cell, this does not mean He *could* not have done so. It indicates that for reasons best known to Him, His purposes are better served by releasing in one instance and by not releasing in another. Or again, if God gave Paul the gift of healing so that he could and did heal others, and yet did not allow him to use that gift on his own thorn in the flesh, this does not mean God's power is not the same. Likewise, if God desired to give the gift of tongues to some in the first century but not even to any thereafter, this in no way indicates that He is not the same.

A second fallacy in this reasoning is the failure to realize that any spiritual gift given only once to one individual in all the history of the church is a gift to the whole church. The gift of apostleship, for instance, was given to a very few, but who today is not still profiting from that gift? Indeed, apostleship and prophecy are said to be limited gifts given only to a few people in the founding era of the church (Eph. 2:20). Actually, since we are no longer living in the founding period of church history, we would not expect God to be giving those gifts which were appropriate to that era. We do not need nor expect to have another cornerstone for the church and neither do we need apostles and prophets today. These belong to the foundation, and we are high up in the superstructure in this twentieth century.

But what about tongues? Was this gift also limited to the early Christians? Hebrews 2:3-4 suggests this: "How shall we escape, if we neglect so great salvation; which at the first began to be spoken by the Lord, and was confirmed unto us by them that heard him; God also bearing them witness, both with signs and wonders, and with divers miracles, and gifts of the Holy Ghost, according to his own will?" Notice that certain spectacular gifts were given to those who heard the Lord ("God also bearing them witness . . .") which were *not* given to the second generation Christians who lived in the first century. Tongues may have been one of those spectacular gifts which was limited in its distribution even within the first century.

3. "Whether there be tongues, they shall cease." This verse

(I Cor. 13:8) plainly states that the gift of tongues will cease to be given. What apparently isn't plainly said is when that did or will happen. And yet there is in the verse itself a strong clue as to when. Three gifts are mentioned in the verse—prophecy, tongues and knowledge (not general understanding, but the spiritual gift; see I Cor. 12:8). The same thing is said about the cessation of two of these gifts, prophecy and knowledge, namely, that they shall be abolished. Exactly the same verb and exactly the same voice of the verb (passive, shall be abolished by someone) is used of both prophecy and knowledge. However, the statement concerning tongues is quite different. The verb is different (*stop*) and the voice of the verb is different (middle). Now we do not have anything quite like the middle voice in English. The nearest expression we have is a reflective (myself, himself). An example of an active voice verb is "The boy *washes* his dog." The passive would read: "The dog *is washed* by the boy." (Prophecy and knowledge will be abolished by God.) If we say, "The dog washes himself" we use a reflective, but in Greek the middle voice would be used. This is what is said about tongues. They will stop or cease of themselves. In other words, God will be obliged to withdraw the gifts of prophecy and knowledge but not so with tongues, for by that time they will have ceased of their own accord. Now if we couple this statement with that of Ephesians 2:20 which says that prophecy was given along with Christ Himself as the cornerstone for the founding of the church, then we may be forced to conclude that tongues (that is, the genuine scriptural gift) died out in that founding era too.

4. There are more important gifts than tongues, and these we are to seek. When the Apostle Paul listed the spiritual gifts in order of importance, he placed apostleship first, prophecy second, teaching third; then miracles, healing, helps, administration; and last in the list, tongues (I Cor. 12:28). Then he said that we are to earnestly desire the better gifts (v. 31). Here is the answer to the question posed in the title of this chapter. Should I seek to speak in tongues? No, I should seek the better gifts. For instance, I should seek to exercise the gift of helps which stands ahead of tongues in the list. This reaffirms what was said earlier about the importance of routine faithfulness as the primary manifestation of true spirituality rather than some spectacular demon-

stration that is like a flash in the pan. If you are concerned about whether or not you should be seeking the gift of tongues, follow this simple and clear teaching of the Scriptures and seek a better gift.

5. Christlikeness does not depend on speaking in tongues. The goal for every believer is Christlikeness, and the fruit of the Spirit is Christlikeness. That fruit, according to Galatians 5:22-23, does not include speaking in tongues or working miracles. Furthermore, as far as we know, our Lord never spoke in tongues, so we can perfectly imitate Him without doing it either. No one need ever feel under pressure that his spiritual life is lacking in some way because he has not spoken in tongues, for Christlikeness does not depend on that. That deep and abiding fellowship with the Lord which we all desire is fostered by increasingly greater knowledge of the Lord, and that kind of knowledge comes through deeper understanding of His Word.

Why all the interest today in speaking in tongues? This is not an easy question to answer. Undoubtedly, for many it relates to a genuine desire to have a deeper experience with God. In some instances a satanic counterfeit is very likely involved, for we know that he is trying to promote orderliness and a kind of godliness in his counterfeit religious experience. I doubt that Satan is willingly or happily involved with fanatics, but he may delight in sidetracking believers from more important activities by leading them into the things we have been discussing in this chapter. The fact that seeming blessing may attend some of these experiences does not necessarily prove that they are of God or that they are the source of the blessing. God may enter any situation and bring good out of it.

Sometimes when students graduate from seminary they miss the Lord's leading and are sidetracked by Satan into a different ministry. And yet during the course of the years they have blessing in this ministry. How does one explain what seems to be blessing outside of the will of God? There are many factors involved in such a situation. Satan did lead them astray. But God rescued the situation and brought blessing to their ministries. And yet such blessing, even from God, does not right the wrong they committed when they missed the leading of the Lord on graduation.

Likewise, some believers miss the best means for fostering their spiritual lives, and yet blessing seems to follow. But, of course, that does not justify using lesser or even counterfeit means to spiritual maturity. If there is any doubt about something as debatable and apparently unimportant as tongues, why not stick to those basic and scripturally clear means of spiritual growth? "Covet earnestly the best gifts."

17

MUST CHRIST BE LORD TO BE SAVIOUR?

ONE OF THE QUESTIONS that inevitably becomes involved in much of the teaching on the spiritual life concerns the lordship of Christ. Sometimes the involvement is accidental; at other times intentional; in any case it is an extremely important question.

THE QUESTION

Simply stated the question is this: Must there be a commitment to Christ as Lord of one's life in order to be saved? Those who answer in the affirmative put it like this: "Those preachers who tell sinners that they may be saved without surrendering to the Lordship of Christ are as erroneous and dangerous as others who insist that salvation is by works."[1] Or, concerning erroneous ways of presenting the gospel to people, another writer asks: "Or will it leave them supposing that all they have to do is to trust Christ as a sin-bearer, not realizing that they must also deny themselves and enthrone Him as their Lord (the error which we might call only-believism)?"[2] Another supporting this same position says, "I am suggesting, therefore, that it is as unbiblical as it is unrealistic to divorce the Lordship from the Saviorhood of Jesus Christ."[3] In other words, if one does not give over the control of his life to the Lord when he receives Him as Saviour, he cannot be saved. Recently there has been a modification of this position to say that *willingness* to be controlled by the Lord at the time of salvation is all that is required in addition to faith in order to be

1. Arthur W. Pink, *Present-Day Evangelism*, pp. 16-17.
2. J. I. Packer, *Evangelism and the Sovereignty of God*, p. 89.
3. John R. Stott, "Must Christ Be Lord To Be Saviour?—Yes" *Eternity* (Sept., 1959), p. 37.

saved. That is, there must at the time of salvation also be a moment of willingness to commit one's life absolutely to the Lord even though the practice of a committed life may not follow completely. But in both variations of this viewpoint the lordship of Christ over one's life becomes a condition for salvation along with faith in Him for forgiveness of sins.

The importance of this question cannot be overestimated in relation to both salvation and sanctification. The message of faith only and the message of faith plus commitment of life cannot both be the gospel; therefore, one of them is a false gospel and comes under the curse of perverting the gospel or preaching another gospel (Gal. 1:6-9), and this is a very serious matter. As far as sanctification is concerned, if only committed people are saved people, then where is there room for carnal Christians? Or if willingness alone is required at the moment of salvation, to what extent is this willingness necessary? Can, for instance, a man who is convinced in his mind that smoking is wrong (not necessarily for spiritual reasons but simply on medical grounds) not be saved until he is at least willing to give up his smoking? Or, what kind of dedication must be preached to people if, in order to be saved, they have already dedicated their lives to the Lord? These are very practical questions about a subject that has important ramifications in many areas.

SOME EXAMPLES OF UNCOMMITTED BELIEVERS

There are in the Bible several clear examples of believers (about whose right relationship to God there can be no question) who were, nevertheless, not completely or continually committed to the Lord. Such examples would seem to settle the issue clearly by indicating that faith alone is the requirement for eternal life. This is not to say that dedication of life is not expected of believers, but it is to say that it is not one of the conditions for salvation. Let's look at these people.

The first two are examples of believers who had definite lapses from a fully dedicated life. They are Peter who said, "Not so, Lord" (Acts 10:14) and Barnabas who, after a successful missionary journey, fell into sharp contention with Paul over whether or not they should take John Mark with them on a second journey (Acts 15:39). Both these men were saved and

serving (Peter's outstanding ministry on the day of Pentecost and Barnabas' service on the first missionary journey are evidence of this); but both rejected the lordship of Christ on subsequent occasions. Now if Christ must be Lord of the life in order for one to be saved, then we are forced to conclude that either Peter and Barnabas were never saved or that they lost their salvation when they rejected the lordship of Christ in these specific instances. Since both men proved quite clearly that they were capable of open rebellion, perhaps we should conclude that they were never genuinely saved.

Of course, many do not wish to come to such a conclusion, and they point out that defection, backsliding, rebellion, or whatever you wish to call it, is possible for a believer. But, they say, it is necessary to have no known areas of unyieldedness when one accepts Christ even though later on in the Christian life backsliding may come into the experience. In other words, at the time of receiving Christ, one must be completely and unreservedly willing to commit his life to Christ as Lord or Master of that life. Momentary willingness is all that is necessary, recognizing that there may be defection later on. How long this momentary willingness must be present in the mind or heart is unclear, but it must be there. The third example deals with this sort of situation.

It concerns those who were converted at Ephesus during Paul's third missionary journey (Acts 19). During the first three months of his stay there, many were converted so that the disciples were separated from the synagogue congregation and taught by Paul in the school of Tyrannus. These converts came out of a background of the worship of Diana (of which worship Ephesus was the center). An important part of this worship included the superstitious dependence on magical words, charms and sayings. These were based on letters which were on the crown, girdle and feet of the statue of Diana in the temple at Ephesus. Magical incantations were compiled in books, and charms were worn as amulets by the Ephesians. Indeed, it is said that a wrestler could not be thrown if he wore his charm, but the minute he took it off he would be overpowered. This is the kind of superstitious background from which the Christians were converted in Ephesus.

In Acts 19:18-19 we are told that more than two years after Paul had first gone to Ephesus "many that believed came, and

confessed, and shewed their deeds. Many of them also which used curious arts brought their books together, and burned them before all men: and they counted the price of them, and found it fifty thousand pieces of silver." It is important to know the tense of the word *believed*. It is a perfect, indicating that those who burned their books that day had believed before that time; that is, sometime during the more than two years Paul had been in Ephesus (see vv. 8 and 10). In other words, they did not burn their books of magic as soon as they had become believers. As believers they had continued to practice and be guided by the superstitious magic of their heathen background. It might be possible to imagine that the very earliest converts in Ephesus did not realize that Ephesian magic was incompatible with Christianity. But it would be very difficult, if not impossible, to say that someone who was converted twelve or fifteen months after Paul had been ministering and teaching there would not have known that if he became a Christian he should do away with amulets and books of magic. And yet apparently many did become genuine believers in Christ knowing that it was wrong to continue to depend on and be guided by their books of magic. Indeed, as far as we know, the book burning was not brought about by preaching against the use of such books by believers, but rather by the fear which followed the judgment on the seven Jewish exorcists who misused the name and power of Jesus. In other words, these believers knew their use of Ephesian superstition was wrong, and when they got a good dose of the fear of God, they did something to right the wrong.

In case I have not been crystal clear about the import of this example, let me say it again. There were people at Ephesus who became believers in Christ knowing that they should give up their use of magic but who did not give it up, some of them for as long as two years after they had become Christians. Yet their unwillingness to give it up did not prevent their becoming believers. Their salvation did not depend on faith plus willingness to submit to the lordship of Christ in the matter of using magical arts. Their salvation came through faith alone even though for months and years afterward many of them practiced that which they knew to be wrong.

The fourth example is one of lifelong rejection of the mastery

of God over a life, and it is the example of Lot. Every time we
see him in the Bible he showed a selfish, unyielded kind of life.
"And Lot was not a high-minded man. With all his early opportunities, and with all his early promises, Lot was not, and never
became, a high-minded man. We are never told all his life one
large-hearted, or one noble-minded, or one single self-forgetful
thing about Lot."[4] If we had only the Old Testament record concerning Lot we would seriously question his spiritual relation to
God. But the New Testament declares that he was a righteous
man in God's sight even when he was living in Sodom (II Peter
2:7-8 where the word *righteous,* translated "just" in v. 7, is used
three times of Lot). So here is a man whose lifelong rejection of
the sovereignty of God over his life did not prevent him from
being righteous in God's sight.

These four examples have shown that temporary unyieldedness
(as with Peter and Barnabas), unwillingness at the time of salvation (as with the Ephesian believers), and lifelong disobedience
(as with Lot) do not keep a man from being righteous before
God. Therefore, we ask, how can the lordship of Christ over
one's life be a requirement for becoming a child of God? I say
again, however, that submission to the lordship of Christ is vital
for a developing Christian life; but becoming a child of God and
growing up to maturity have different requirements, and lordship
over the life is not a requirement for getting into the family of
God.

The Meaning of Lord

But, someone may ask, doesn't Lord mean Master, and doesn't
receiving Jesus as Lord mean as Master of one's life? To be sure,
Lord does mean Master, but in the New Testament it also means
God (Acts 3:22), owner (Luke 19:33), sir (John 4:11), man-
made idols (I Cor. 8:5), and even one's husband (I Peter 3:6).
When it is used in relation to Jesus in the New Testament, it can
have an ordinary meaning of a title of respect (as in John 4), but
it must also have had some unusual connotation which caused
some to question its validity. And such a meaning could only be
God. In other words, when someone who apparently was no
more than an ordinary man from a poor carpenter's family

4. Alexander Whyte, *Bible Characters: Adam to Achan,* p. 131.

claimed to be God, and when the title Lord, which meant "Jehovah-God" to the Jewish mind, became attached to this Man
Jesus in the preaching of the apostles, then there was division.
Such division would not have been so sharp if Lord Jesus meant
merely "Sir Jesus" or "Master Jesus"; but if it meant "God Jesus"
or "Jehovah Jesus," then one can account for the division and debate over that kind of claim.

If Lord means God and Lord Jesus then means the God-Man,
notice some ramifications of this concept. In I Corinthians 12:3
Paul said, "No man can say that Jesus is the Lord [literally, Lord
Jesus], but by the Holy Ghost." Lord in this sense must mean
Jehovah-God for the simple reason that unsaved people can and
do say Lord, meaning Sir, in reference to Christ, before they
even have the Spirit of God. Furthermore, how could Peter have
been led by the Spirit to say, "Not so, Lord [Master]" (Acts 10:
14)? Did the Spirit lead him to utter such a contradiction? But,
of course if Lord meant God in such a statement, that makes
sense, for one can recognize the deity of Jesus without being
willing to admit His sovereignty over a particular matter, and
that's exactly what Peter did.

Why is Lord Jesus (meaning God-Man) such a significant
statement that it can only be said by the Spirit of God guiding
a person? It is because this is the essence of our salvation since
it focuses on the uniqueness of the Saviour. Almost all "saviours"
claim mastery over the lives of their followers. There is nothing
unique in Christ's relationship with His followers if that is all
Jesus the Master means. Even the leaders of cults claim this.
But what religion, other than Christianity, has a savior who
claimed to be both God and Man in the same person? If Lord
in the phrase Lord Jesus means Master, then the claim to uniqueness is absent. If Lord in the phrase Lord Jesus means Jehovah-
God, then Jesus is unique, and this is the very heart of the message of salvation in Christianity.

As the average person observed and listened to Jesus of Naza-
reth preaching and teaching, he was not offended by what he
considered to be simply another man, even another prophet.
Nor did it trouble him that this Jesus claimed the allegiance of a
band of twelve or of seventy or even more disciples. But what
did cause division among the people was His claim to be God as

well. Not a man who claimed to be master, but a man who said he was God is what angered them. The Jews clearly said on one occasion, "For a good work we stone thee not; but for blasphemy; and because that thou, being a man, makest thyself God" (John 10:33). The offense is the God-Man, not the Master-Man.

Why is this such a crucial matter in our salvation? It is for the simple reason that no other kind of savior can save except a God-Man. Deity and humanity must be combined in order to provide a satisfactory salvation. The Saviour must be a man in order to be able to die and in order to be identified with the curse on man. And He must be God in order that that death be effective for an infinite number of persons. When Paul wrote of the gospel to the Romans, he said that it concerned God's Son, Jesus Christ, and then he elaborated only two essential facts about Jesus Christ— His humanity ("made of the seed of David according to the flesh") and His deity ("declared to be the Son of God with power" [Rom. 1:1-4]). He did not add anything about Christ's sovereign control over the lives of those who accept Him as an essential part of the gospel. It was not until chapter 12 that Paul addressed believers concerning the matter of dedication. The God-Man saves; the Master controls and sanctifies.

This same emphasis is seen in Romans 10:9: "That if thou shalt confess with thy mouth the Lord Jesus . . . thou shalt be saved." It is the confession of Jesus as God and thus faith in the God-Man that saves from sin. This is the same point that Peter drove home on the day of Pentecost when he said: "Therefore let all the house of Israel know assuredly, that God hath made that same Jesus, whom ye have crucified, both Lord and Christ" (Acts 2:36). Jesus the Man had been proved by the resurrection and ascension to be Lord, God and Christ, the Messiah. They had to put their faith in more than a man; it had to be in One who was also God and the promised Messiah of the Old Testament.

This is what Peter meant by repentance when he was asked by the people what they should do in the light of his message (Acts 2:38). The word *repent* means, of course, to change one's mind about something. But what that something is is all-important to the meaning of repentance in any given context. A criminal may be repentant in relation to a mistake he made, intending to change his mind not about his general character but only about

the conduct of his profession so that the next time he will not make that mistake. Christians need to repent about specific sins in their lives (II Cor. 7:10). The content of repentance which brings eternal life, and that which Peter preached on the day of Pentecost, is a change of mind about Jesus Christ. Whereas the people who heard him on that day formerly thought of Jesus as a mere man, they were asked to accept Him as Lord (Deity) and Christ (promised Messiah). To do this would bring salvation. It is true, too, that repentance about sins may lead an unsaved man to turn to Christ; but being sorry for sins or even changing one's mind and thus his life will not *of itself* bring salvation. There must also be a change of mind about Jesus Christ so that He is believed and received as personal Saviour from sin.

An Analogy

Does this emphasis on the deity of Christ mean that the phrase Lord Jesus includes no other connotations in the term Lord? Definitely not, but it does mean that deity is the principal emphasis and the focal point of faith as far as salvation from sin is concerned. To be sure, Lord includes other ideas.

But let's not pursue that for the moment. Rather, let's look at the name Jesus. All agree that this is the human name of our Lord and emphasizes His being a real, but perfect, human being. Since God cannot die, faith in Jesus, the Man who could and did die, is necessary for salvation. The Saviour has to be a Man (because divine judgment rests upon man), and that Man was Jesus. Thus the name Jesus focuses attention on the human Person who died. But, of course, the humanity of our Lord is important in relation to some other things. For instance, it is Jesus, the human Person, who is held up to the believer as an example for his own life and service (I Peter 2:21; I John 2:6). Christ's example is important, yes, vital; and it is related directly to His humanity. But this is not part of the gospel. When I ask men to receive Jesus as their Saviour, I am, in using the name Jesus, trying to face them with the One who died for them, not One who is an Example for living. While the concept of example is implicit in the name of Jesus, this is not the issue in salvation. Even lordship preachers do not make it so.

Furthermore, the humanity of our Lord is important in the second coming. "This same Jesus, which is taken up from you into heaven, shall so come in like manner as ye have seen him go into heaven" (Acts 1:11). "They shall look upon me whom they have pierced" (Zech. 12:10). The human Jesus is the One who will come again, but does a person have to believe in Jesus, the coming One, in order to be saved? No, for the message of salvation concerns Jesus, the dying One.

Now, if in using the name Jesus in preaching the gospel, we only emphasize His humanity as it relates to His dying and we do not emphasize His humanity as an example or as related to His return, then is it wrong to insist that Lord as it is used in the gospel message emphasizes His deity and not the many other aspects or characteristics of God?

For example, the Lord God is also the Creator. Must one believe that the Lord is his personal Creator in order to be saved? Or again, the Lord is the Judge. Must one believe in Christ as the One who will judge him in order to be saved? Or again, the Lord is the Sovereign of all things. In order to be saved must one acknowledge Him as the Sovereign of his personal life any more than he should acknowledge Him as the Sovereign of Israel or of the world or of the millennial kingdom? In other words, if the gospel of the Lord Jesus includes lordship over my life, it might very well also include the necessity of believing He is my Creator, Judge, coming King, Example, Teacher, and so forth, on and on, to include every attribute of Deity and every aspect of the perfect humanity of the Lord Jesus. While the words Lord Jesus do not exclude any of these things, the emphasis the Bible gives to these words (as we have tried to show from Acts 2, for instance) is on His being the God-Man, Man in order to die, and God to make that death effective for the remission of sins. Where do you stop if you start adding something else to this which is the gospel revealed in the Bible? If you add lordship over life, what right have you to include only that? And if you add to the gospel other ideas included in the word Lord, why not add the other ideas included in the name Jesus? And, of course, if you do any of this, you complicate the gospel beyond comprehension and effectiveness.

THE MEANING OF DISCIPLESHIP

Actually to teach that Christ must be Lord of life in order to be Saviour is to confuse certain aspects of discipleship. What is a disciple? A disciple is one who receives instruction from another; he is a learner. In the New Testament the word is used frequently in the Gospels, occasionally (by comparison) in Acts, and not at all after Acts. There were disciples of Moses (John 9:28), of John the Baptist (John 3:25) and of Christ. Of Christ's disciples some were only temporary and deserted Him after a time (John 6:66); some were closer to Him (Peter, James and John); one was a traitor (Judas). Judas, of course, is an example of an unsaved disciple; thus the word *disciple* does not necessarily imply true conversion. However, usually the word is used of converts and in the book of Acts it becomes a synonym for *believer*.

Now making disciples is the objective of the Great Commission (Matt. 28:19). Two things characterize Christian disciples—they are baptized (a clear sign of their faith in Christ) and they are constantly learning. Baptism is a single event, but learning is a lifelong process. What is testified to in baptism can be accomplished by an act of faith. What is taught in the "all things whatsoever I have commanded you" cannot be fully accomplished in an entire lifetime. There is one condition for baptism—faith (Acts 16:31-34); there are many conditions for growth. Confusion enters when we attempt to take the conditions for growth and make them conditions for becoming a disciple, or when we make the characteristics of the life of discipleship conditions for becoming a disciple.

The Lord distinguished these two facets of discipleship—the entrance into discipleship and the life that follows—in two side-by-side sermonettes. In Luke 14:16-24 he related the parable of the great supper into which entrance was unrestricted, free and for all. In Luke 14:25-33 He taught the restrictions of the life that continues to follow Him in the ongoing process of discipleship. To make the conditions for the life of discipleship requirements for becoming a disciple is to confuse the gospel utterly by muddying the clear waters of grace of God with the works of man.

Incidentally, it is worth noticing that the characteristics of discipleship require action, not merely willingness to act. Therefore, the variation of lordship teaching, mentioned earlier, which says that a man to be saved has to accept Christ and at least momentarily be willing to submit to Him, could not be substantiated by these verses. If, for instance, Luke 14:33 could be conceived as stating conditions for salvation, the verse does not say that we must only be willing to forsake all; it says we must forsake all. Or again, if Matthew 19:21 is how to be saved, the Lord did not tell the young man merely to be willing to sell all; He told him to do it.

THE EASE OF BELIEF

As said earlier, the teaching that salvation is by grace through faith alone in the God-Man Saviour as our Substitute for sin has been dubbed "easy believism." It is not true, however, that those of us who believe this deny that it is also important to enthrone Christ in one's life. We are saying that enthronement is not a condition for salvation but rather that it should be a consequence of it. But the question still remains, Is that label "easy believism" a true one? Is it really easy to believe? Consider two arresting thoughts.

1. The object of our faith involves unbelievable demands. He is Someone unseen; He lived in the distant past; the contemporary records about Him were preserved by His friends; and there are no living eyewitnesses today who could verify the truth of His claims. Is it easy to believe someone like that? Credit is a big business all over the world today, but credit is extended to people only with some safeguards. We often look the person over; we collect information about him; and in some cases we ask others to vouch for the person. None of these things are available to those whom we ask to believe in Jesus. To be sure, there are records about Him, but some say they are not reliable. And there are those who claim to have been wonderfully redeemed by Him, but they may have been deluded. Is it really easy to believe in the unseen Christ?

2. The content of our faith involves unbelievable demands. We are asking people to trust this unseen Person about forgiveness of sins and eternal life on the basis of the death of that

Person which is said to be substitutionary. Is that easy? If we were asked only to trust Christ to direct the affairs of this life, that is not so crucial, for we might have a seemingly and relatively happy and successful life without His control (though, of course, it can't compare with a life that is lived under His control). But we dare not risk missing the forgiveness of sins; for eternity, not merely a few years of life, is at stake. When all of this is poured into the content of our faith, can we say it is easy to believe?

May I conclude with an illustration? Years ago with another student I was on a train going from Athens to Istanbul. Somewhere along the line a nice-looking man boarded who began to engage me in conversation. It was a difficult conversation because our only common language was French; but eventually it came through to me that he wanted to exchange some Turkish money for American dollars. Now these were the days of free exchange rates so it was perfectly legal, and the dollar was a very desirable commodity. Naturally I was wary of this stranger who wanted money, but as the hours wore on and we neared Istanbul we agreed to meet that evening in the hotel where my friend and I would stay. The semi-cloak-and-dagger scene that night in that third-class hotel was almost comical as I look back on it. My friend and I each sat on one of the two iron beds in the small room; the man with the money brought his brother (so he said) along, and they sat on two straight chairs (the only other furniture in the room). After the usual pleasantries, we got down to bargaining. Of course I had done some checking that afternoon on the going rate, so in due time we agreed on the exchange which, as it turned out, gave us our stay in Turkey at a 25 percent discount. The bills were exchanged; we said good-bye; and that seemed to be the end of that.

A few weeks later, due to unforeseen circumstances, my friend and I had to separate and I was obliged to return to Scotland alone. Because of the unexpected change of plans, I needed to buy a plane ticket out of Istanbul. So when I got back there, I decided to look up my money changer (whose address I had taken for some unknown reason) and see if I couldn't buy that ticket at a 25 percent too! Five streets off the boulevard and six flights up I found his apartment and knocked at the door. The

brother appeared (and indeed he was), and soon the three of us were reminiscing about our previous meeting. Well, I said, that same problem had brought me back that night—I needed more Turkish money. Did he, perchance, need more dollars? Yes, he did, and as his story unfolded it came to light that he himself was a refugee from a communistic Balkan country who had fled to Turkey. But his wife and family had been settled in Canada by one of the world relief agencies because she was a medical doctor. Having no profession he had not been able to go with them, but his consuming ambition in life was to bring his family to Turkey so they could be together again. To do this required stable currency like dollars, but it was not easy to transmit them to his wife. He would like to help me himself, he said, but . . . .

I had a suggestion. Would he meet me in the morning, buy my ticket for me, and then trust me to write my father in the United States and ask him to send the equivalent amount from my account there to his wife in Canada? Do you get the picture? I was asking him to trust me (whom he really did not know) to reimburse him from an account which I claimed to have in a distant country through a father whom he had never seen and concerning whose existence, let alone honesty, he had no way of checking on. Would he do it? Would he believe me? His decision was not an easy one, for I was making unbelievable demands on his faith.

Well, he did, and of course I kept my part of the bargain. In due time the dollars went to his wife, and this was what enabled the family to begin the process of reunion. Eventually they were together again, and grateful letters from both the husband and his wife are among my prized possessions. Is it easy to believe?

If you are ever tempted to add something to the uncomplicated grace of God, first try making it crystal clear who is the Object of faith and what is its content. Then point men to Him, the Lord Jesus, the God-Man Saviour who offers eternal forgiveness to all who believe.

18

THE BALANCED CHRISTIAN LIFE

IF I WERE GIVEN MORE to the spectacular I would entitle this concluding chapter "The Secret of Success in the Spiritual Life" or
"The Formula for the Victorious Life" or something similar. I
have the suspicion, however, that the "formulas" and "secrets"
contribute to the problems people have rather than reveal solu-
tions. "Try this," says one; "Try that," says another. The result
of these many voices and general lack of agreement on what
really are the biblical means to Christian maturity seems to be
breeding two kinds of believers. There are some who are not
quite sure that they are even on the right track of normal Christian living; there are others who are quite certain that they have
arrived at the station! Or, to change the metaphor, there seem
to be so many master chefs around that some are so confused by
looking only at the various menus that they are starving to death,
while others are sampling everything that is offered with re-
sultant indigestion, and a few have sworn allegiance to one and
are convinced that all the others are frauds!

In this chapter we want to do three things: (1) summarize and
chart some of the routes, (2) push the station farther down the
track so that no one may think that he has arrived, and (3) illu-
minate the track so that all can see what are the biblical means to
maturity and thus live a balanced Christian life.

VARIOUS EMPHASES

When one attempts to summarize and chart the emphases
among the various teachings on the spiritual life, there is always
the danger that comes with oversimplification. Nevertheless,
setting things side by side can also bring clarification, and that's

our aim. Let it be said, too, that in listing these various emphases
I am not suggesting that the entire teaching is wrong; it contains,
in my judgment, an imbalance because some aspect of the spiritual life has been emphasized in a manner disproportionate to
the place given to it in the Scripture.

First, there is the view which emphasizes the idea that God
does all that needs to be done for us in the spiritual life. We not
only can do nothing; we must do nothing; otherwise we will
hinder the work of God in our lives. Usually this decision to let
God do it all comes as a crisis point in one's experience; it is then
that we learn to "let go and let God" which is the secret of a victorious life.

It is not our purpose to elaborate here on the difficulties in
these overemphases; hopefully, that has been done in the preceding chapters. Suffice it to say that of course God must do the
work in and through us, but we must play our proper role in
sanctification as well. Charted, this emphasis looks like this:

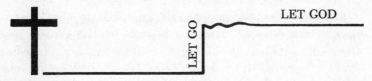

To be sure, there may be some ups and downs on the level of the
higher life, but these are relatively small after one has experienced
the yieldedness crisis.

While this first concept emphasizes the crisis dedication aspect
of the spiritual life to the minimizing of the fight aspect, a second
variation focuses attention on the continuous fight and excludes
any teaching on a definite break with sin in an act of dedication.
Charted, it appears like this:

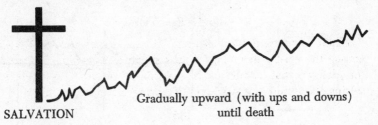

A successful fight will lead to a gradual but certain conquering of the sin nature and, in some variations of this idea, to an eradication of it.

Of course, there is a straightforward eradication viewpoint that teaches that the sin nature is completely removed at a crisis experience when one meets the conditions of the particular group teaching it. This is a sudden eradication, while the previous variation teaches that a successful fight leads to eventual eradication. Diagramed, the "sudden eradication" view looks like this:

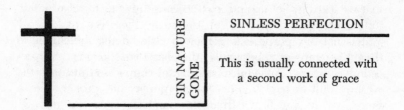

Another viewpoint emphasizes continual or repeated dedications or revivals as the means to spirituality. Such teaching misses the point of the tense of the verb used, for instance, in Romans 12:1 for "present." It implies an event, not a succession of events, as discussed in chapter 7. To be sure, after a decisive or crisis act of dedication there may be experiences of backsliding. However, the remedy for this is confession and often a reaffirmation of that initial dedication. Call it rededication if you will, though this is not a good term to convey the biblical teaching; but do not hold out a series of rededications as the desired thing in the Christian life or as something which in any way demeans that all-important initial, decisive and complete act of dedication. Diagramed, the teaching looks like this:

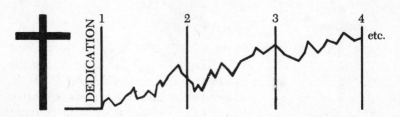

Finally, I should mention an emphasis which one runs into occasionally. It's the idea that the chief means to sanctification is what is called openness. This involves a great deal of public and group confession both as a catharsis and as an incentive to better living. We have already discussed the subject of confession in chapter 14, so that need not be repeated here. But today this misemphasis sometimes takes the form of group self-analysis usually directed by someone who has been through the process successfully. These "self-discovery" sessions (sometimes even with a series of checklists) are supposed to lead one into maturity of some sort. I say "of some sort" because my impression is that often emotional maturity is substituted by these groups for real spiritual maturity, and it is not a substitute, desirable as it may be. It seems too as if the goal is little more than learning to accept oneself with all one's faults and foibles through this process of gaining freedom to talk about these personal things in front of a group.

Of course there is a place for knowing oneself and seeking emotional stability in one's life, and sometimes group interaction can help. But what seem to be lacking in this movement—and these are basic and crucial lacks—are, first, an objective standard against which to measure self and, second, an appropriation of the power of the indwelling Spirit to make the changes necessary to pursue Christlikeness. What really is accomplished as far as achieving biblical spirituality is concerned if one only learns to accept his own quirks or even gains acceptance by others? God Himself as revealed through His Word is the standard by which we must measure ourselves, and not some checklist. Then changes must come—changes in us personally, not merely changes in a group's acceptance of us. Only then are we on the right road to spiritual maturity. (It seems impossible to diagram these ideas helpfully!)

ACHIEVING THE GOAL

Achieving the goal of the Christian life is a continuous and lifelong process. Simply stated the goal is Christlikeness, but the full realization of this awaits our ultimate glorification (Rom. 8: 29-30). For anyone to assert that he has arrived in the Christian life, he must be able to say (and to back it up with constant

proof) that he is Christlike. Even if one could live in this life without sin (which is not possible), he would also have to manifest the positive characteristics of our Lord, for Christlikeness is more than the absence of sin.

But we can be achieving the goal in this life even though we cannot arrive at it until we are translated to heaven, and there are many exhortations in the New Testament that urge us to keep on. "But grow in grace, and in the knowledge of our Lord and Saviour Jesus Christ," urged Peter, and that word *grow* is in the present tense indicating a continual process of growth. There never comes a time for any Christian when he does not need to grow more in the Christian life. John reminded us that the blood of Christ "cleanseth us from all sin" (I John 1:7)—another present tense indicating the continuousness of our need. Paul indicates that the new man is constantly being renewed (another present tense) throughout life (Col. 3:10). In the light of these verses it is quite clear that no one has arrived in the Christian life. Someday we all will by the grace of God; in the meantime we keep on pursuing the goal set before us.

THE RIGHT TRACK

What is the right track to genuine spirituality? What are the factors that make up a balanced formula for Christian growth? In my judgment there are four, and while they have been discussed in one way or another in the previous chapters of this book, it may be helpful to put them together in a final summary form.

1. Dedication. Before any lasting progress can be made on the road of spiritual living, the believer must be a dedicated person. Although this is not a requirement for salvation, it is the basic foundation for sanctification. As we have pointed out, dedication is a complete, crisis commitment of self for all of the years of one's life. Such dedication may be triggered by some problem or decision that has to be faced, but it concerns a person, the child of God, not an activity or ambition or plan for the future. A dedicated person will have dedicated plans and ambitions; but dedicated plans do not necessarily require or guarantee dedication of the planner.

Dedication is a break with one's own control over his life and

a giving of that control to the Lord. It does not solve all the problems immediately and automatically, but it does provide the basis for solution, growth and progress in the Christian life. In other words, if one dedicates his life to the Lord in, say, an evening service, he does not wake up the following morning with all his problems solved. But he does have a firm basis for solution. Any "formula" for victory which pictures dedication as suddenly and automatically lifting one to a higher plane of experience is misleading. It is not this way:

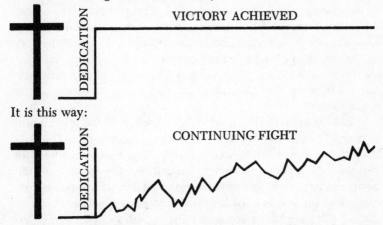

It is this way:

God can work with yielded lives, but the job is then only just beginning. Other things are necessary after dedication.

2. The second element in a balanced view of the spiritual life is discipline. Paul wrote: "if ye through the Spirit do mortify the deeds of the body, ye shall live" (Rom. 8:13). This is a very interesting verse which brings a great deal of balance into the spiritual life. For one thing, it declares that those who have already crucified the flesh (Gal. 5:24) still need to put to death the deeds of the body. The tense is present, signifying something that needs to be done repeatedly even though we have been crucified (aorist tense indicating a completed event). For another thing, this verse declares that *we* do this—through the Spirit to be sure, but nevertheless, *we* have a vital part. "You" is the subject of the verb *put to death,* and it is in the active voice. *I* do it. If it were a passive voice then it would mean that someone else does it for me. The Holy Spirit enables, but *I* do it. This is

a hard fact to bring into any view of the spiritual life that pictures God as doing it all, but the verse is quite clear.

What does it mean to "put to death"? Death always means separation, never extinction, so putting to death the deeds of the body cannot mean eradicating them. That doesn't happen in this life. But it does mean separating myself from these things. Death, I said, means separation. Notice: physical death is the separation of the material and immaterial, but not the extinction of either. Spiritual death is separation from God, but not extinction of the human being who is spiritually dead. The second death is also separation from God but not extinction even in the lake of fire. Death to self is not extinction of the self-life but separation from its power. So putting to death the deeds of the body does not mean that those deeds will no longer be a part of our existence, but it can mean that they need not be any longer a part of our experience.

What are some of the "deeds of the body"? There is a biblical answer to this in Colossians 3 where the same word *deeds* (v. 9) is used and some of those deeds listed. Notice some of them. In verse 5 are listed several things that fall into the category of unclean matters, especially in the realm of sex. Fornication, uncleanness, passion and bad desires—these are unclean deeds of the body from which a spiritual believer will be separated. Certainly this means no participation in such things; does it also mean separation in our reading and viewing?

Another practice which belongs to the old is covetousness (v. 5), and here, as elsewhere in the New Testament, it is called what it really is—idolatry. Recall chapter 8 about money and remember that covetousness does not automatically disappear when one has more money. One can be covetous when he has little, much, or anything between, for covetousness comes from the heart, not from the circumstances of life.

In verse 8 are mentioned sins of speech. These too are deeds of the body from which the spiritual believer will be separated. They are wrath, anger, malice, blasphemy and abuse. Sometimes those who seem to be the most spiritual fail to manifest any control in this area of the tongue and thus belie their supposed spirituality.

Discipline in the areas of the flesh, money and speech is an

essential part of spiritual living, and that disciplining is something I must do.

3. The third facet of a balanced spiritual life is dependence. "This I say then, Walk in the Spirit, and ye shall not fulfil the lust of the flesh" (Gal. 5:16). Constant dependence on the power of the indwelling Spirit of God is essential to spiritual growth and victory. By its very nature, walking is a succession of dependent acts. When one foot is lifted in order to place it in front of the other one, it is done in faith—faith that the foot that remains on the ground will support the full weight of the body. You can walk only by the exercise of faith. You can live the Christian life only by dependence on the Holy Spirit. Such dependence will result in the Spirit's control over the deeds of the flesh (Gal. 5:17-21) and the Spirit's production of the fruit of the Spirit (vv. 22-23).

Dependence on the power of God and effort on the part of the believer are not mutually exclusive. Self-discipline and Spirit-dependence can and must be practiced at the same time in a balanced spiritual life. Dependence itself is an attitude, but that attitude does not come automatically; it usually requires cultivation. How many genuine Christians there are who live day after day without even sensing their need of dependence on Him. Experience, routine, pride, self-confidence all tend to drag all of us away from that conscious dependence on God which we must have in order to live and act righteously.

4. Finally, the spiritual life must be a life of continual development. No verse expresses this so well as I John 1:7 (though it seems an unlikely proof of this at first glance): "But if we walk in the light, as he is in the light, we have fellowship one with another, and the blood of Jesus Christ his Son cleanseth us from all sin." The standard for all Christian conduct is God Himself (v. 5). God never lowers or compromises this standard. He is the criterion by which all conduct and attitudes and goals are measured. That is why sin may be defined as coming short of the glory (or manifestation) of God (Rom. 3:23). In this pragmatic generation and rationalizing society it is well to remember this. But, you say, we can never meet this standard; so isn't God mocking us with an ideal which we cannot hope to achieve? The answer is no; for while the standard is God Himself, the require-

ment for every believer is to walk in the light (v. 7). We are
not expected to become light but we are expected to walk in the
light. Now this is a requirement which all can be expected to
meet, for it is tailored to each Christian's stage of maturity at all
times. The standard, light, is fixed and unchanging; the requirement, to respond to the light, is different and attainable in each
case. The areas of life into which the light of God and His Word
shines are always expanding in the process of growth of the normal Christian life. This is true of physical growth and it is true
of spiritual growth.

If we walk in the light, two consequences follow: we have
fellowship with other believers *and* the blood of Christ keeps on
cleansing us. For a long time I unconsciously read the verse this
way: If we walk in the light we have fellowship with one another, but if we don't walk in the light the blood of Christ
cleanses us. But this is not what the verse says. It declares that
we need cleansing when we are *in* fellowship with the Lord, not
when we are out of fellowship. Constant cleansing, therefore, is
a consequence of walking in the light.

What does this mean? It means simply this: When we are
walking in fellowship with the Lord, the light of God's Word
shines on additional areas of our lives and shows up our sins
and frailties which then need the cleansing power of the blood
of Christ in order that we may continue to walk in the light.
These may be areas that come to light in the normal course of
growing up physically and/or spiritually. For instance, as a Christian child I was not concerned with the question of whether or
not I would serve the Lord; when I did give my life to the Lord,
where I would serve Him was not an issue; before I had children,
the question of whether I would give them to the Lord, as much
as a parent can, was not an issue. All these things arose in the
normal progress of life, and as they came up and I reacted positively to the will of God, the blood of Christ kept on cleansing
me from all sin. This is the cleansing that relates to growth, not
the cleansing that results from confessing known and deliberate
sin (I John 1:9).

This is the normal development of the Christian life. Walking
in the light brings additional light and cleansing of those previously darkened areas. As we then walk in the light that includes

those added areas, more areas of life come under the searchlight of God. Walking (by us), enlightening (by the Word), cleansing (by the blood)—this is the repeating cycle of Christian development.

This is the road of spiritual life—a dedicated life that is disciplined, dependent and developing. This is the "secret" of spiritual success; and yet it is no secret, being plainly revealed in God's Word. The difficulties that face all of us are two: keeping the various facets of the truth in proper balance, and then doing what we know is necessary.

Hopefully this book has helped with the first. May the Lord help us all with the second.

Moody Press, a ministry of the Moody Bible Institute, is designed for education, evangelization and edification. If we may assist you in knowing more about Christ and the Christian life, please write us without obligation to: Moody Press, c/o MLM, Chicago, Illinois 60610.

SELECTED SCRIPTURE INDEX

Prepared by Rev. Joel T. Andrus

OLD TESTAMENT

GENESIS
3:1-24 26
4:4 27
4:8 27
39:1-23 141

DEUTERONOMY
15:16-17 77

ISAIAH
14:14 125

MALACHI
3:1-18 88

NEW TESTAMENT

MATTHEW
5:14-15 132
5:21-26 148
6:12 150
6:13 140
6:14-15 150
13:24-30 126-27
18:21-35 148-49
19:21 179

LUKE
8:4-15 107
13:7 55
14:16-24 178
14:25-33 178-79
18:1-8 105-6

JOHN
7:37-39 120
13:1-17 149
14:20 49
15:4 49
16:13 11
16:19-31 54

ACTS
1:4 113
1:5 113
2:36 175
2:38 175
10:14 170, 174
10:45 114
11:15-16 113-14
15:19-29 157
15:39 170
19:11-20 142
19:18-19 171

ROMANS
1:11 99
2:29 40
5:12 50
5:12-21 28
6:1-10 53, 56
6:6 55
6:11 56
6:14 151
6:18 161
6:18-20 35
6:22 161
7:15-25 35, 45-46
7:18 34
8:6 35
8:13 65, 187-88
10:9 175
12:1 75, 184
12:1-2 79-81
12:2 38, 83
12:7-8 96
13:14 141-42

I CORINTHIANS
2:12 11
2:14 44
2:15 12-13
2:16 37
3:1-2 15
3:1-5 19
3:1-7 18
3:3 19
6:11 61
7:31 155
7:36-39 47
8:13 156, 161
10:13 138-39
10:31 30, 102, 157
11:19 19
12:3 174
12:13 51-52, 113
12:28 96
12:31 97-98, 166
13:8 166
14:5 164
15:22 50
15:44 44
16:2 85-87

II CORINTHIANS
2:11 128
4:4 36
5:17 34
8:4 85
11:27-32 73
12:7-10 131

GALATIANS
2:20 16, 33, 55, 65
5:13 161
5:16 65, 114-15, 189
5:17 35
5:22-23 16, 116-18, 167
5:25 35

EPHESIANS
1:17 114
3:13 104
4:3 18
4:12 99
4:26 145
5:18 13, 111-12, 121
5:18-21 21
5:20 17
5:22 21
5:23 22
5:24 22
5:25 22
5:26-27 62
5:29 22
6:11-18 133-34

PHILIPPIANS
4:8 39

COLOSSIANS
2:12 53
3:5 188
3:8 188
3:9 35, 188
3:10 186
4:2 70

I THESSALONIANS
2:18 127
5:17 70
5:23 45

II THESSALONIANS
2:8 54
3:13 106

I TIMOTHY
4:1 128
5:14-15 128
6:6 91
6:10 92
6:11 91

II TIMOTHY
2:22 143
3:5 126

TITUS
2:4 95
3:11 19

HEBREWS
2:3-4 165
2:11 63
2:18 139
3:8 41
3:13 41
4:12 41
4:14-16 41
5:10-11 17
5:13-14 20
13:7 158
13:17 44, 158

JAMES
1:2 140
1:12 140
1:23 67
4:7 132

I PETER
1:6-7 136-37
1:14 80
1:16 61
2:2 66
2:21 16

II PETER
2:7-8 173
2:19 161

I JOHN
1:7 186, 189
1:8-10 31
2:1 130
2:6 16
2:15 156
3:1-3 62
3:4 30

JUDE
19 44
24-25 62

REVELATION
2:24 128
12:11 132
20:10 55